TOLLUND MAN

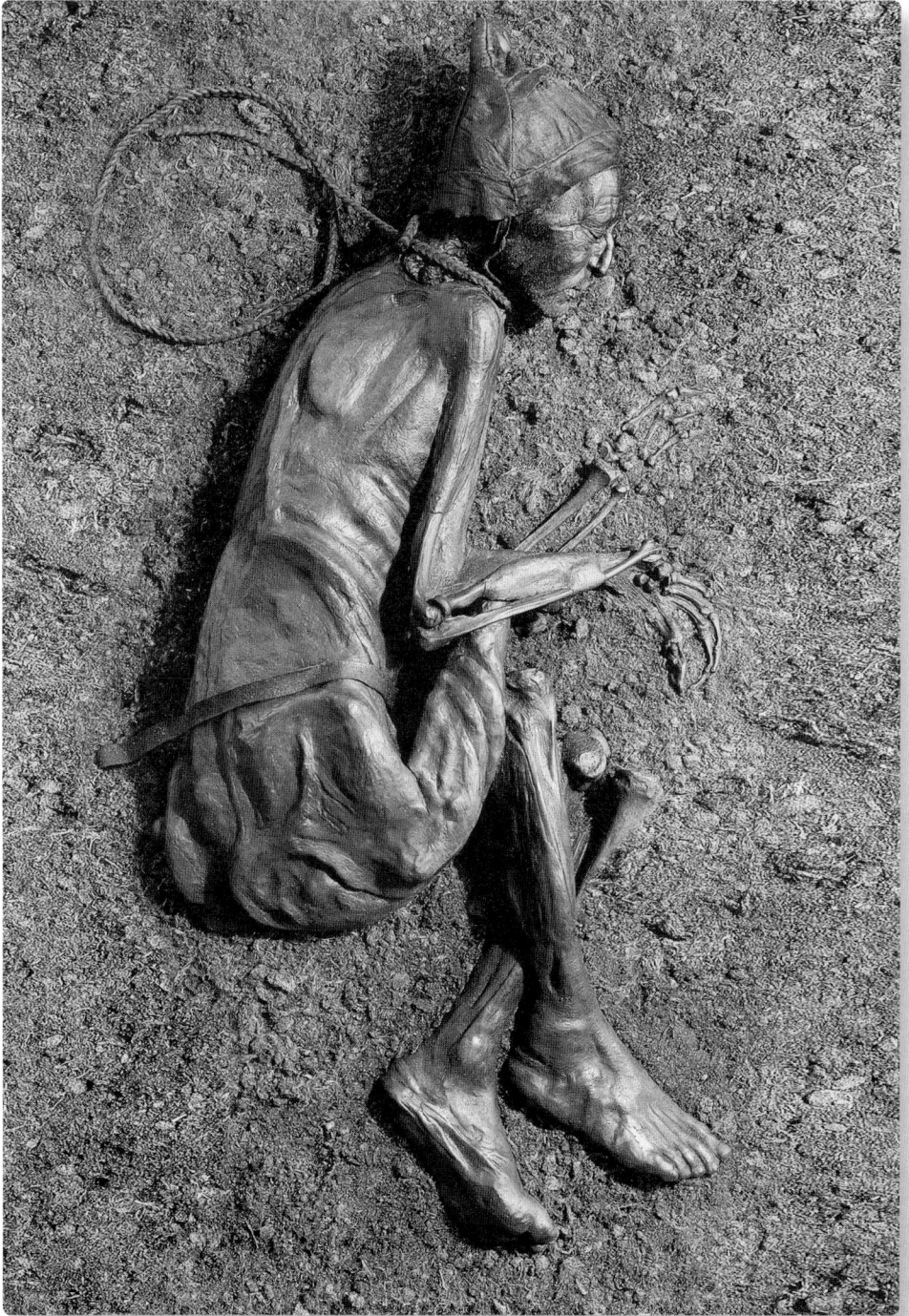

TOLLUND MAN
GIFT TO THE GODS

CHRISTIAN FISCHER

The
History
Press

> from The Tollund Man
>
> Bridegroom to the goddess
>
> She tightened her torc on him
> And opened her fen,
> Those dark juices working
> Him to a saint's kept body ...
>
> Seamus Heaney, 16th October 1973

Seamus Heaney's poem 'The Tollund Man', as he wrote it in Silkeborg Museum's visitors' book.

Cover images courtesy of Silkeborg Museum and Robert Clark.

First published in Danish by Forlaget Hovedland 2007
This English language edition first published 2012

The History Press
The Mill, Brimscombe Port
Stroud, Gloucestershire, GL5 2QG
www.thehistorypress.co.uk

British Library Cataloguing in Publication Data.
A catalogue record for this book is available from the British
Library.

ISBN 978 0 7524 8635 2

Typesetting and origination by The History Press
Printed in Great Britain

CONTENTS

Acknowledgements

Following the publication of the Danish edition of this book, the author was awarded two major prizes: the Westerby Award for science and communication and the Bergsøe Foundation's prize for communication and presentation of scientific work. The need for an English translation was a view expressed from many quarters. Thanks and recognition are therefore due to archaeological scientist Dr David Earle Robinson and archaeologist Anne Bloch Jørgensen for producing this English version.

Museum curator Karen Margrethe Boe has provided invaluable assistance both with respect to its specialist content and in proofreading.

The History Press and editor Tom Vivian are thanked for their willingness to publish this edition and for their cooperation throughout.

INTRODUCTION

The term 'bog people' has become a popular concept and the bog men from Tollund and Grauballe are now firmly established in our historical consciousness. This is due primarily to the late Keeper of National Antiquities P.V. Glob's book *The Bog People*, which was published in 1969 and has become a classic text in archaeological literature. Worldwide bestseller lists at the time bear witness to Glob's abilities as a writer and to the subject's universal appeal. Artists and writers all over the world, including the Nobel Laureate for Literature, Irish poet Seamus Heaney, consider *The Bog People* to be one of their greatest sources of inspiration.

Producing a new book dealing with the same subject is consequently rather a risky undertaking, but the subsequent fifty years have yielded so much new information that much of the data from that time now requires revision. New technology in archaeology, medicine, physics and chemistry has made it possible to get even closer to the people of the Iron Age. Since the publication of Glob's book, the period from which most of the bog bodies originate has been narrowed down considerably, to between *c.* 500 BC and AD 1 – the so-called Celtic or Pre-Roman Iron Age; the former term will be employed in this book.

Human corpses from distant prehistory are found in many places around the world where the vagaries of nature result in organic material being preserved. The phenomenon results from various physical and chemical conditions, for example cold in Greenland and the Alpine glaciers, dry air in the Andes Mountains and in the deserts of the Sahara and Taklimakan, salt in the mines at Salzburg and the tanning properties of north-west Europe's oceanic raised bogs – which created the bog bodies.

P.V. Glob's book *The Bog People*.

This book deals primarily with the Danish bog bodies, specifically Tollund Man and Elling Woman, who were both discovered in Bjældskovdal in Central Jutland. The other Danish bog bodies mentioned here were chosen according to the information they could contribute, with particular attention being given to preserved soft tissues and attendant clothing and artefacts. As far as I am aware, no examples have been excluded which contradict the interpretation presented here.

Christian Fischer
Silkeborg Museum, April 2012

1

6 MAY 1950

Every archaeological discovery has its own story and this story can often overshadow that of the actual finds – for better or for worse.

In 1639, when Kirsten Svendsdatter of Møgeltønder came across the first of the renowned Danish golden horns, she asked for a petticoat as a reward. Hans Lassen found the second golden horn in 1734 and he believed himself deserving of aquavit. The golden horns became properly famous when, in 1802, they were stolen, providing inspiration for Denmark's most renowned poet, Adam Oehlenschläger. Any information the horns could provide on prehistory receded into the background.

The reward for one famous find, the Late Bronze Age gold vessels found at Borgbjerg Banke near Sorø, resulted in the family responsible being able to pay for their son to train as a vet and, on this foundation, their grandson was subsequently able to crown his political career as Minister of Education. Appropriately, the family took their new surname – Borgbjerg – from the find site. Their beneficial discovery was of gold – the situation could be quite different when the find was a bog body, which was only recognised as being something completely unique and of great scientific importance many years later.

The discovery of Tollund Man in 1950 did not change the lives of the finders. They continued their modest existence and were more or less forgotten while others, in glossy magazines and on television, presented the man from the bog to an astonished world.

Someone who has followed the story very closely is John Kauslund, whose parents and paternal uncle made the original discovery. He remembers the day for several reasons; it was his eleventh birthday that eventful Saturday. He was his mother's firstborn and, following the death of his father at the end of the Second World

War, she had remarried, to Viggo Højgaard. John then gained two siblings, Ada and Ole, aged six and one, respectively, in 1950.

In 1950 rural society in particular was still suffering the consequences of the aftermath of the Second World War; there was a lack of commodities, fuel, well-paid work and good housing.

John's birthday began like any other day in that everyone rose at about 6 a.m. and there were the usual daily morning chores to do. John, who was now big enough to wield a fork, and his stepfather Viggo went out into the byre to muck out and feed the animals. The hens also had to be fed and the milk churns put out

Bjældskovdal at the beginning of the 1950s. *(Photo: J. Troels-Smith)*

so they could be collected and taken to the dairy. Then the main task of the day, peat cutting, would begin. This had to take place in May and June as the cut peats had to be laid out in the sun to dry.

His mother Grete was in the kitchen preparing oatmeal with milk and making up packed lunches so work in the peat bog would not be interrupted in the middle of the day by returning home to eat. Sandwiches – white bread with homemade jam – and juice, made with berries from the garden, would take the edge off the worst of the hunger during the day.

Just after 7 a.m., the two horses Grå (Grey) and Røde (Red) were hitched to the four-wheeled cart. It took just less than an hour to drive from their home at Sejlgårds Mark to the peat cutting in Bjældskovdal. They had previously lived in Tollund, which was closer to the bog, but the farm there had been sold and they had moved on. John's uncle still lived in Tollund, where the family home had been. The family retained turbary rights (the right to cut turf) on the lot owned by John's grandmother Nicoline. Virtually all the farms in the district – large and small – had a peat lot for their own use. There were also large peat contractors and merchants who sold the peat further afield.

The cart set off with baby Ole lying in his pram on the back. Ada, who acted as his babysitter, had the job together with John of preventing the pram from sliding around, or worse, as they drove down the rutted gravel tracks which led via a sunken road to the bog. This was a road which probably had its origins in the ancient Hærvej – a network of drove roads that extended down through Jutland from Viborg to Schleswig. Down in the bog the family met up with Uncle Emil, and they got to work. One of the first tasks was to find a cool place to store their food and drink during the day. But the bog was always cold once you dug just beneath the surface.

The horse Grå was not very good at pulling in the bog so it was tethered, and Røde was hitched to a small cart which ran on rails. The two adult men stood in the bog and cut the peats with a special spade. These were then placed on a board on the cart and hauled by Røde up to Grete, who transferred them from the cart to the drying ground. She then placed an empty board on the cart and sent it back down to the peat cutters. It was John's job to cut up the peats which were laid out to dry. When fairly dry, after about a month, they were piled up into beehive-like stacks to continue drying and then later they were carted home. The men of the Højgaard family cut peat for themselves and two siblings. Home on the farm, the peats filled up a cart shed. As well as heating the house, they were also fuel for the stove used every day for cooking.

At the time, in May 1950, the newspapers were reporting that the government intended to relax fuel rationing. Peat cutting for small households was on the way

One of the sunken roads at Bjældskovdal. *(Photo: Silkeborg Museum)*

out and by 1953 most of Denmark's small bogs lay more or less abandoned as scarred natural landscapes. The prevailing smell in towns changed from acrid peat smoke to that of coal and coke. However, as late as the 1960s, the author carried peat briquettes in every day for the stove in the family's holiday house.

Grete kept a watchful eye on the peat cutting. According to John, she was a remarkable woman who broke with convention by taking part in the work. She had lived a tough life and had had to work hard in order to survive. Her temperament and her 'man's work' set her apart and this was not appreciated by everyone in the small local community.

It was almost lunchtime, John recalls, when Uncle Emil's peat spade struck something. It could have been a branch or a tree root such as they had encountered

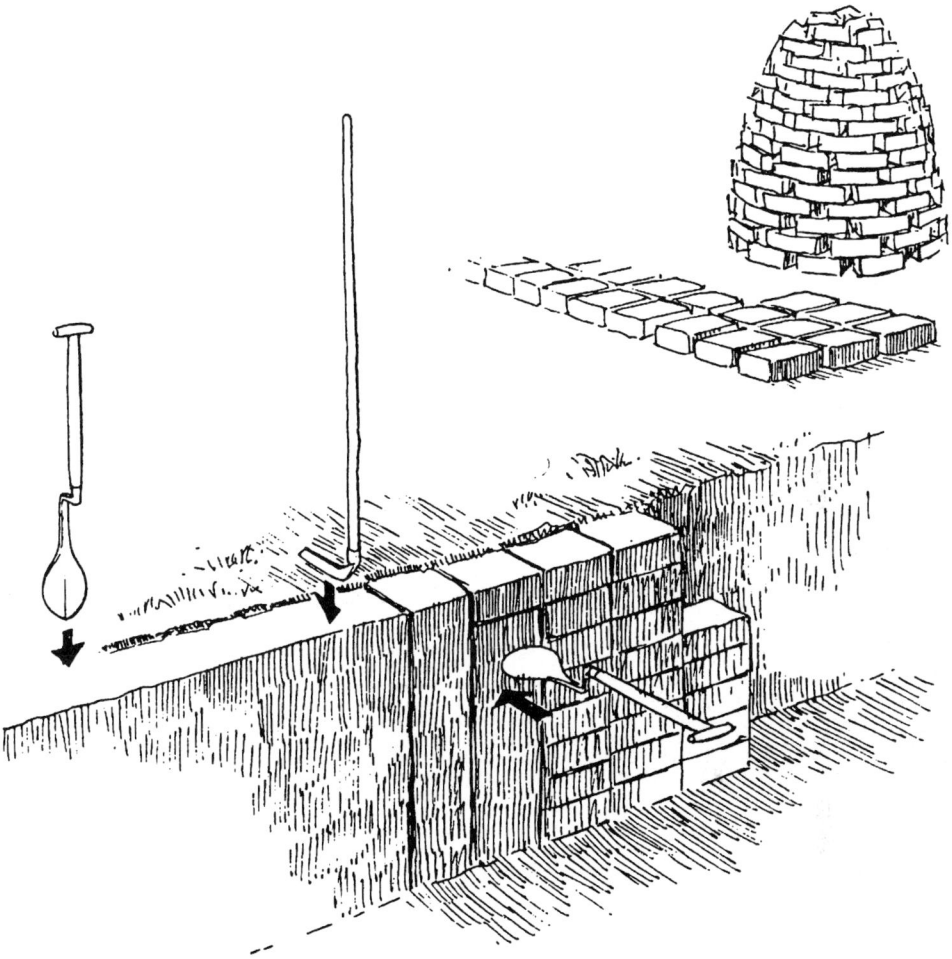

Cutting and stacking peats. 1. A deep strip of peat is cut free of the baulk. 2. The strip is cut into columns. 3. The columns are divided up into individual peats. 4. The peats are laid out to dry on the drying ground. 5. The peats are stacked to complete drying. (*Reconstruction drawing: Flemming Bau*)

so often before, but Grete was immediately aware of the situation. 'What's going on?' she asked. She apparently had some sixth sense because she continued, 'Be careful, it could be something exciting'. Emil, who had struck 'something' and who had a temperament to match Grete's, responded that it was probably a tree stump, and a loud and lively discussion ensued.

A couple of days earlier, they had found a wooden implement during the peat cutting. This looked like a short sword with a transverse handle fixed to it.

Grete Højgaard surveys the recently revealed corpse at the base of the peat cutting. *(Photo: Niels T. Søndergaard)*

A few years previously, a similar discovery had been made at a bog, Nørre Smedeby Mose, in Southern Jutland of implements which told the story of peat cutting during the Early Iron Age. The Højgaard family were obviously not the first cutters of peat in Bjældskovdal.

Abandoning further discussion, Grete uncharacteristically left her work unloading the peats and, just as unusually, she told John to go with her down the 50m to where the men stood, more than 2m deep in the peat. John was, however, ordered to keep his distance. Grete rolled up her sleeves and kneeled down – and shortly afterwards she exclaimed: 'You can say what you like, but there is

Viggo and Grete Højgaard at the find site. *(Photo: Niels T. Søndergaard)*

"something" under here.' John was only 4–5m away when his mother proclaimed that she had her finger into 'something'. A little later, after she had removed some peat with her hand, it turned out that her finger had gone up between the forehead and the skullcap of a human corpse. Shortly afterwards the entire Højgaard family stood face to face with a small well-preserved human head – Tollund Man had been discovered!

After they had recovered their composure a little, the question occurred: Was this a body from prehistory or that of a recent murder victim? Never before had they found a corpse in the bog, human or animal. However, not far away, probably only about 40m, a body had been found previously – in 1938 – but the Højgaard family

Professor P.V. Glob in the bog. The horse Grå in the background. *(Photo: Probably P.V. Glob himself)*

didn't really know much about this. They were, though, very aware of another case. Many local people had taken part in the search for a school boy, Henning Carøe Jensen from Hvidovre near Copenhagen, who had disappeared not long ago while on a cycle trip through Central Jutland. His route may well have passed in the vicinity of Bjældskovdal. Could it be him? The uncertainty nagged at them and in order to find out whether or not this was something criminal, Grete telephoned the police in Silkeborg to inform them of their discovery – but that was not until the Monday as the family did not have a telephone.

The case was dealt with by DS Traugaart Zschau and DI K.G. Kristiansen, nicknamed 'the Fox'. Kristiansen was famous for his ability to ferret out clues and was widely renowned for solving the murder of priest and poet Kaj Munk, who was liquidated by German henchmen in 1944 at Hørbylunde Bakke, not far from Bjældskovdal. In addition to being a very shrewd detective, Kristiansen also made up one third of the leadership team for Silkeborg Museum, which at that time was run on a voluntary basis. Before they left the police station for the crime scene, he made sure they were joined by another expert in museum matters, chief librarian Peder Nielsen. They were almost certain that the case would not prove to be a recent one as the corpse was overlain by several metres of undisturbed peat. It was Nielsen and Kristiansen's knowledge of archaeology which meant contact was swiftly made with Professor P.V. Glob. The previous year he had been appointed to Aarhus Museum and the University of Aarhus as the university's first professor of archaeology. They asked Glob to come to the site as quickly as possible. He arrived that same day, 8 May. This date is often erroneously given as the date on which Tollund Man was found, but he was of course discovered two days earlier, on 6 May – John's birthday.

P.V. Glob had recently completed excavating a Neolithic village with burial sites located at Barkær on Djursland, and at the same time an important Iron Age war booty site had also been found at Illerup, near Skanderborg.

Although many bog bodies had been found over time prior to this, very few had ever been investigated scientifically. The reasons for this ranged from peat cutters considering it best to rebury their discovery as quickly as possible so as not to be involved in a fuss (police and archaeologists), to the purely practical circumstance that it was simply not possible to notify the authorities. During the war, fuel was in short supply and there was an urgent need to cut and dry the peat, or have it macerated and mixed if it was not suitable for cutting into blocks. Even power stations were dependant on this home-produced resource. If, when they found something, the cutters did stop work in order to notify the authorities, news of the discovery would have been passed to the nearest archaeological museum, the

Professor P.V. Glob on his way to the find site with his excavation gear.

National Museum in Copenhagen, and it was permanently understaffed. If the museum had enough resources to investigate the find, wartime travel restrictions would also have hampered their efforts, and days could elapse before any of their staff reached the find site.

Finds of bog bodies were therefore, in numerical terms, at an all-time low during the war, even though peat-cutting activity was at its height. After the war, when the need for peat was not quite so pressing, the number of reported finds rose before falling again during the course of the 1950s, when peat production more or less came to an end. Just after the war, reports often came in from families like the Højgaards, who cut peat for their own consumption and for whom an archaeological discovery could mean a break in the work, but would cause minimal inconvenience.

The Højgaard brothers had continued to cut peat around the body so that when Glob and his companions arrived at the site it lay uppermost in a block of peat. They could see the outline of a person lying on their right side, head to the west and facing south, towards dry land on the bog margin. It was also clear that a femur had been fractured by a spade during peat cutting. It was decided to recover the body the next day, even though Professor Glob would not be able to be attend; if they delayed it might suffer some form of damage. They were aware that the body needed to be kept wet, but if it remained unprotected then rot and fungi would rapidly take hold, so speed was of the essence.

A photograph taken on 8 May shows that Glob brought along the usual archaeological instruments – tape measures and theodolite – to survey in the find. However, whether he used these instruments is uncertain as there is apparently no survey data from that day.

Glob probably concentrated his efforts on giving advice so that the body could be excavated under the best possible circumstances. In several places the texture of the find was similar to that of a digestive biscuit after it had been dunked in a cup of tea. Accordingly, the correct approach was to recover the body as it lay within the supporting peat – as a block – so that it could then be excavated under optimal conditions, i.e. at the National Museum's Department of Conservation in Copenhagen.

Glob instructed that a wooden crate needed to be constructed around the body and so Grete and John, who had just arrived home from school, set off on their cart to visit carpenter Ejner Lunding at his workshop in the vicinity of the bog near Funder Kro, an inn which was a landmark on the road from Aarhus to Ringkøbing. The carpenter was rather shocked when Grete asked for planks for a man-sized coffin. Grete was not just anybody. However, the planks were soon on their way to the bog where quite a crowd had gathered. This included people from Silkeborg Museum and policemen who, although off-duty, wanted to follow the 'case' to its conclusion. The press were also there and two of Silkeborg's newspapers reported on the find. Only *Silkeborg Social-Demokrat* made it front-page news; *Silkeborg Avis* contented itself with just a paragraph on an inside page while *Venstrebladet* made no mention of the discovery.

It was erroneously reported by the press that the body was wrapped in a fur coat and that a ham had been placed close by. The 'fur coat' can probably be explained by the fact that the body lay in a kind of peat referred to as 'dog flesh' which is

Velbevaret oldtids-fund i mosen ved Moselund!

S. S. & S. 5

Voksent menneske afdækket under torvegravning

Silkeborg.

UNDER tørvearbejde i mosen, der ligger mellem Elling og Moselund, blev der i lørdags gjort et interessant fund af et velbevaret menneskeskelet, der sandsynligvis stammer fra oldtiden. Man vil forsøge at faa professor G l o b fra Nationalmuseet til at se paa fundet, som man haaber kan indlemmes i museumssamlingen i Silkeborg.

De to brødre Viggo og Emil Højgaard er beskæftiget med tørvegravning i mosen, og det var husmand Emil Højgaard, Tollund, der i lørdags stødte paa skelettet. Han dækkede det straks til, og i formiddag blev politiet i Silkeborg underrettet.

Kriminalassistent K. G. Kristiansen, der er en stærkt interesseret oldtidsforsker, tog i formiddags til mosen bl. a. sammen med overbibliotekar Peder Nielsen, Silkeborg.

Man stod overfor et velbevaret fund, der sikkert stammer helt tilbage fra oldtiden. Noget drab eller en anden kriminel handling har der ikke været tale om.

Kvinde fundet paa samme sted

Det ser ud som om mennesket, der er voksent, er blevet begravet, idet liget tilsyneladende er gyet ind i noget tøj. Det ligger sammenbøjet med knæene trukket op under hagen. Fundet blev gjort i tørvejorden i ca. 2½ meters dybde.

Muligvis har der været en gravplads det paagældende sted, idet man for 7—8 aar siden afdækkede skelettet af en kvinde, der laa begravet ca. 50 meter fra det sted, hvor det nye skelet nu er fundet. Man kunne dengang med det samme konstatere, det drejede sig om en kvinde, idet hendes haar laa velbevaret, og ogsaa paa det nye fund kan man se haaret.

Man søger nu at faa fat i professor Glob, der i øjeblikket befinder sig paa Djursland efter at have besigtiget de nye store mosefund paa Skanderborg-egnen. Fra lokal side haaber man stærkt paa, at det nye fund maa blive indlemmet i Silkeborg museumsforenings oldtidssamling.

Fundet, der er gjort ved Moselund, er dækket til, da det let kan blive ødelagt, saafremt det udsættes for luftens paavirkninger. Der er saaledes ikke noget at se for uvedkommende, og man opfordrer egnens befolkning til ikke at give sig til at grave paa stedet, da det kan forvolde uoprettelig skade   b o y.

A newspaper cutting reporting the discovery.
(Silkeborg Social-Demokrat, 8 May 1950)

very fibrous. 'The ham' was probably the femur which had been fractured by the peat spade and therefore protruded somewhat. The newspapers told their readers that the find had been covered over as it could easily suffer damage if exposed to the effects of the air. It was emphasised that there was nothing to be seen for unauthorized persons and the local population was encouraged not to begin digging at the site as this could cause irreparable damage.

According to the newspapers, a wooden spade with a short transverse handle was found a few metres from the corpse. Unfortunately, this object, although photographed for the press, was not preserved. It does, however, provide further confirmation of later palaeoecological observations made in the bog to the effect that the body had been deposited in a prehistoric peat cutting.

Tollund Man was found in the bog's fibrous 'dog flesh' peat. It was therefore – mistakenly – believed he was wrapped in a fur. *(Photo: Niels T. Søndergaard)*

The newspapers reported that curiosity at the site was so overwhelming it led Nielsen to break his own rules and touch the body:

> ... strictly speaking there should have been no further contact with the corpse before its journey to Copenhagen. However, during the strenuous work on Tuesday afternoon the team of volunteer workers were given the opportunity of a tiny glimpse of the uppermost part of the head as chief librarian Peder Nielsen, with extreme care, lifted enough of the peat to reveal, among other things, the remarkable brow furrows. Apart from this, the entire afternoon was taken up with rather monotonous digging and the extremely difficult task of building the crate around the body.

The hope was also expressed that the new discovery could be incorporated into Silkeborg Museum Society's prehistoric collection.

It was Silkeborg Museum's staff who, according to Glob's instructions, directed the work involved in cutting down around the body to create a block of peat the length and breadth of which was slightly greater than the outline of the body itself. The crate was lowered down around this block and the base planks were pushed in underneath – one at a time through the peat – then firmly screwed to the sides. A layer of damp peat – like that in which the body lay – was then placed over and around the corpse. Once more planks had been screwed on to form a lid, the body lay secure, cushioned in the peat, and the crate with its contents could be carefully taken away.

It was not possible to use a crane or a cart to move the crate and so the now large crowd of spectators – who had not followed the newspapers' request to keep away – were summoned into action. The very heavy crate was loosened and hauled out manually from the peat cutting to the waiting cart, pulled by Røde and Grå. It was exhausting work and the many volunteers included several policemen among their number; Silkeborg Avis mentions a total of ten. One of the policemen became unwell during the lift and, suffering from heart problems, had to be helped from the site. He died a couple of days later from the over-exertion.

Once the crate was on the cart, Grete and John could set off for Moselund railway station, from where the route led on directly to the National Museum. The journey to the station went by way of Femørevejen – a private road running across the southern end of the drained Bølling Lake. From time immemorial, people who were not plot owners had been able to use this road in return for payment of a 'toll' of 5 øre. The transport of Tollund Man took place, however, free of charge.

Spectators at the find site. The finders and the children John and Ada with little Ole in Viggo's arms. *(Photo: Unknown)*

The following day the newspapers optimistically report that: 'The prehistoric find from Moselund arrives at the National Museum today'. However, the trip ended up taking a total of eight days.

At some point the corpse was given the name Tollund Man. We don't know for sure who was responsible. It is usual to name archaeological finds after the place

Tollund Man being packed into a crate which was assembled board by board around him. From left to right: chief librarian Peder Nielsen, DI K.G. Kristiansen and (wearing a hat) stationmaster Holger Hansen. *(Photo: Unknown)*

Oldtidsfundet i Moselund til Nationalmuseet i dag

s. s. 9. 6. 50

Professor Glob har undersøgt fundet, som er ca. 2000 aar gammelt

Silkeborg

DET oldtidsmenneske, som er fundet i mosen mellem Elling og Moselund, menes at være ca. 2000 aar gammelt. Det er velbevaret, og arkæologer har iagttaget visse interessante ting ved fundet, bl. a. ser det ud til, at oldtidsmennesket har haft et bælte omkring livet og at et stykke oksekød med skank i sin tid er gravet ned sammen med liget. I dag bliver fundet gravet op og sendt til Nationalmuseet i København til grundig undersøgelse. Præpareringen vil vare mange maaneder, men naar den er overstaaet og fundet klarlagt, haaber Silkeborg museumsforening paa, at oldtidsmennesket bliver overladt til det lokale museum, der magler et egentligt, samlet fund af den art.

Man gaar meget omhyggeligt til værks, naar fundet tages op af tørvemosen. Rammerne til en stor kasse graves ned omkring skelettet. Saa bliver bunden sat paa, kassen fyldes op med mosejord omkring skelettet, saa sættes laaget paa, og det hele køres til København.

Professor Glob fra Nationalmuseet undersøgte fundet i aftes sammen med interesserede, stedlige arkæologer. Som nævnt i gaar er mennesket (man ved endnu ikke, om det er mand eller kvinde) meget velbevaret, ikke mindst takket være, at de to brødre, Emil og Viggo Højgaard, der stødte paa skelettet under deres arbejde i mosen, har udvist stor forsigtighed.

Man kan tydeligt se ansigtets form og den ene fod, der har været helt afdækket. Kun bækkenpartiet har taget lidt skade, da en spade har ramt det.

Dyreknogle ved liget

Det drejer sig om et saakaldt moselig, af hvilke der i aarenes løb er fundet et halvt hundrede stykker i Jylland, Nordtyskland og Holland. Det er ikke sjældent, at saadanne lig har været genstand for en voldsom behandling. Den døde kan findes bagbundet, sammensnøret eller krumbøjet omkring en nedrammet pæl.

Foreløbig har man ikke i Moselund kunnet se tilstrækkeligt til, om oldtidsmennesket har været udsat for overlast. Det ligger i en sammenkrummet stilling med knæene trukket op under hagen.

Almindeligvis blev moselig dengang iklædt en kappe paa overkroppen, men intet paa underkroppen, og noget tyder paa, at det menneske, der er fundet nu, har baaret en saadan klædning, men der er det pudsige, at det ser ud, som om den døde har baaret et bælte om livet, og det var ikke almindeligt for den tids mennesker. Det er umuligt paa nuværende tidspunkt at se, om der har været en spænde i bæltet.

En anden pudsighed ved fundet er, at det ser ud, som om der er nedlagt mad til den døde ved begravelsen. Der findes nemlig ved liget en knogle, som ikke stammer fra et menneske, men som sandsynligvis er en okseskank.

Som omtalt blev en kvinde fundet i den samme mose ikke langt fra det nye fund for 7—8 aar siden. Man ved endnu ikke, om der har været en gravplads i mosen.

b o y.

Husmand Emil Højgaard, Tollund, staar i mosen, hvor han stødte paa oldtidsmennesket, der ligger til højre for hans fødder, dækket til med mosejord, saa luft ikke kan komme til skelettet.

Professor P. V. Glob i færd med at undersøge det interessante fund.

Newspaper cutting reporting the journey to the National Museum. *(Silkeborg Social-Demokrat, 9 May 1950)*

Liget i Tollund Mose er 2000 Aar gammelt

5. G. 9. 5. 50

Et uhyre velbevaret Jernaldermenneske, der i Dag føres til Konservering paa Nationalmuseet

Silkeborg

DET arkæologiske Ligfund, der, som omtalt, blev gjort forleden i Funder, blev i Gaar besigtiget af Professor Glob. Professoren ankom sidst paa Eftermiddagen til Silkeborg, og sammen med Overbibliotekar Peder Nielsen, Kriminalassistent K. G. Kristiansen og Stationsmester Hansen tog han til Mosen i Tollund, hvor Brødrene Viggo og Emil Højgaard, Tollund, havde fundet et Menneske, indsvøbt i Faareskind. Undersøgelsen paa Stedet blev dog kun af ganske kort Varighed og havde for saa vidt kun det Formaal, at Professoren skulde konstatere, at der virkelig var Tale om et Moselig. Det kunde fastslaas omgaaende, lige saavel som det tydeligt fremgik, at Fundet er uhyre velbevaret.

Prof. Glob

Om det er en Mand eller Kvinde, er man endnu ikke klar over, men Professoren vil skønsmæssigt anslaa dets Alder til omkring 2000 Aar. Paa denne Baggrund vil man forstaa Forbløffelsen over, at man endnu kan se Panderynkerne. Ansigtet er i det hele taget, ligesom den ene Fod det mest velbevarede paa Liget. Professoren traf paa Stedet Beslutning om, at Fundet straks skal føres til Nationalmuseets Konserveringsanstalt,

og allerede i Dag sker Forsendelsen. De nævnte lokale Museumsfolk foretager i Eftermiddag, assisteret af frivilligt Mandskab, bl. a. flere Politibetjente, den særdeles vanskelige Pakning. Liget er som nævnt lagt tilbage til Stedet, hvor det blev fundet, og ved Pakningen lader man hele Jordklumpen, der omgiver det, følge med.

Overbibliotekar Peder Nielsen udtaler overfor AVISEN, at de to Findere har vist den alleryderste Forsigtighed, for at der ikke skulde ske Fundet de mindste Overlast, og det paaskønner Arkæologerne og Museumsfolkene i høj Grad. Brødrene Højgaard opdagede Liget, da den enes Spade stødte mod noget haardt, som man først antog for en Træpind. Det viste sig at være Laarknoglen af Jernaldermennesket.

Det hævdes, at der for 7—8 Aar siden blev gjort et tilsvarende Fund i Nærheden, men Overbibliotekaren udtaler, at dette i hvert Fald aldrig er naaet til Museumsforeningens Kundskab. Nu haaber Foreningen, at det skal lykkes at bevare dette Fund for Silkeborg Museumsforening, hvilket der skulde være gode Chancer for.

Newspaper cutting with Professor P.V. Glob's statement. (*Silkeborg Avis, 9 May 1950*)

where they were discovered, i.e. the Skuldelev Ships, the Jelling Stones, the Hoby Beakers and so on. The area where the bog body was found is known, rather un-dramatically, as Bjældskovdal or Moselund. However, as the finders lived, or had previously lived, in Tollund, then this more dramatic-sounding name was chosen, even though the village is located about 1km away. My personal guess as to the identity of name-giver is P.V. Glob, who had a legendary ability to promote an understanding of the importance of an archaeological find. Tollund means Thor's grove, and 'that's real history', I can almost hear Glob say.

Two years later, in 1952, another bog body was found near Silkeborg. This time the bog was Nebelgaard Mose and, just like Tollund Man, this body also came to be known by a different name – Grauballe Man – even though Grauballe is located some distance from the find site. But the village was the home of the peat cutters and Glob was again in attendance.

On his visit to the find site in Bjældskovdal, Glob told the newspapers that the body was 2,000 years old. A few years previously, he had directed the National Museum's excavations at Borremose in Himmerland and, in addition to the remains of a fortified Iron Age village, three bog bodies were discovered there over a period of three years. One of these, found in 1946, had clothing with stitching corresponding to that which Glob could see on Tollund Man's cap. With the aid of pollen analysis, a method believed capable at the time of providing an exact date, the body from Borremose had been assigned to the Early Roman Iron Age, a period which begins around AD 1.

2

EXCAVATION AT THE
NATIONAL MUSEUM

After Tollund Man had been sent off by train from Moselund railway station, destined for the National Museum, life for the Højgaard family continued as usual and they resumed their peat cutting in Bjældskovdal.

At Silkeborg Museum they waited excitedly for news from the great museum in Copenhagen. The team involved in the day-to-day running of Silkeborg Museum and responsible for all practical aspects – from excavations to the gluing together of potsherds and dealing with correspondence – comprised three gentlemen, known collectively as 'The Triumvirate'. In the bog we made the acquaintance of chief librarian Peder Nielsen and DI K.G. Kristiansen and they were accompanied in the actual recovery of the body by stationmaster Holger Hansen, whose knowledge of archaeology and excavations was renowned far and wide. But if money or legal aspects were involved in any way then the chairman of the Museum Society, barrister Otto Bisgaard, took charge. Towards the end of May everyone's patience was at breaking point and Bisgaard wrote the following letter to the National Museum:

As you are probably already fully aware by way of a communication from Professor, Dr P.V. Glob to Senior Curator, Dr Therkel Mathiassen, a bog body was discovered early this month in Tollund. On the recommendation of Professor P.V. Glob, the entire find was sent in a large crate to the National Museum's Conservation Department, where we hope it arrived in good condition.

As we would like to be able to exhibit the find at Silkeborg Museum, we are very interested to know how much the conservation will cost.

I can inform you that Silkeborg Museum will in the current year acquire premises at Silkeborg Hovedgaard and will accordingly be in a position to exhibit such a find which can be expected to stimulate interest in the museum significantly here in the town where, as I am sure the National Museum is aware, we are in possession of a very extensive archaeological collection.

The circumstance that the find was discovered in the close vicinity of Silkeborg, in conjunction with extensive press coverage of which it has been the subject, has awakened great interest for museum matters in Silkeborg and environs. Consequently, it is the Museum Society's hope that at some time in the near future it will be possible to exhibit the find at Silkeborg Hovedgaard.

With all due deference
On behalf of the committee

The following day, senior curator Therkel Mathiassen, head of the National Museum's Prehistoric Department, sent a reply. For Silkeborg Museum this must have felt like a slap in the face:

In reply to your letter of the 25th of this month, I can inform you that it is quite correct that some time ago we did receive the bog body from Tollund, but no accompanying description, so we have been in some doubt as to what the intention was with it. Neither have we received a report from Professor Glob apart from the fact that, during my visit to Aarhus the other day, he told me that he had been involved in its recovery. We would be pleased to receive a report from the person responsible for the recovery of the body. I am familiar with the location of the find site through discussions with stationmaster Hansen, Bording.

I see that Silkeborg Museum wishes to exhibit the find conserved in its entirety. However, I am not sure that this would be a good idea. It is quite a macabre sight and, furthermore, most of the body is so poorly preserved that it will be very difficult to conserve. The only possibility of which we are aware at present with respect to conservation of a body such as this is to place it in water to which has been added a preservative fluid. But given the present state of the body, it can only decay further and the water will become murky and unpleasant. Our conservators are presently working on the problem and it is possible that a solution can be found. Otherwise I believe we will have to suffice with simply retaining the head, which is exceptionally well preserved with facial expression etc., as well as the leather cap, the cord and the belt; and we will of course conserve these for Silkeborg Museum. If it is only these parts which are to be prepared, the National Museum will not charge for the actual work but only for the costs of the container and the fluid, and this will probably not be a major item.

But as already stated, the problem has not yet been completely clarified, just as the find has yet to be fully examined.

Yours sincerely,

Therkel Mathiassen

Apart from revealing that Glob had not written a report on the discovery, the letter shows that aesthetic considerations were also taken into account with respect to

The excavation at the National Museum took place outside, in the museum's courtyard. *(Photo: Lennart Larsen)*

optagelsen af liget. Selve findestedets beliggenhed kender
jeg gennem samtale med stationsforstander Hansen, Bording.

Jeg ser, at Silkeborg Museum ønsker fundet udstillet
som præparat. Jeg er dog ikke sikker på, at dette vil være
heldigt. Det er jo et temmelig makabert syn, og desuden er
det meste af liget så dårligt bevaret, at det vil være meget
vanskeligt at konservere. Den eneste mulighed, vi i øjeblikket
kender, til at bevare et sådant lig er at lægge det i vand
tilsat en konserverende vædske. Men sådan som ligets tilstand
er, vilde det flyde ud og vandet blive uklart og uappetitligt.
Vore konservatorer arbejder nu med problemet, og det er muligt,
at der kan findes en løsning. Men ellers tror jeg, vi må
nøjes med at opbevare hovedet, som er fortrinligt bevaret med
ansigtstræk o.s.v., samt skindhuen, snoren og bæltet; og disse
dele skal vi nok konservere for Silkeborg Museum. Hvis det
kun bliver disse dele, der skal præpareres, vil Nationalmuseet

Korrespondance bedes adresseret til I. Afdeling uden Angivelse af Personnavn.

Therkel Mathiassen, head of the National Museum's Prehistoric Department, writes: '... very macabre sight ... just conserve the head ...' and leaves no doubt that the find belongs to Silkeborg Museum.

the conservation of the body. They would 'suffice' with only preserving the head (which would actually make the greatest demands with respect to conservation) so that it could be exhibited at Silkeborg Museum. The preservation and exhibition of the entire specimen was advised against because of the inherent practical difficulties of conservation and the fact that it would result in rather a 'macabre sight'.

Reassuringly, the charge to Silkeborg Museum for conservation of the head would only amount to the cost of a container and chemicals. The container later proved, incidentally, to be saucepan.

The National Museum's letter was followed by several further missives from Silkeborg Museum. The first of these was sent at the end of May and in it chief librarian Peder Nielsen declares himself in agreement with Therkel Mathiassen with respect to the impossibility of exhibiting the find in its entirety, judging from the press photograph taken during the excavation of the peat block at the National Museum. The picture was published in the newspapers *Jyllands-Posten* and *Silkeborg Social-Demokrat* on 27 June 1950, and it was indeed a very macabre sight. Again it is important to note here that aesthetics were heavily involved in the decision with respect to conservation – if this had been a bent, rusty iron sword there would be no doubt that it should be preserved as it was – science demanded it. It is a source of some wonderment today that it did not occur to anyone that the side of the body which faced downwards in the bog was just as well preserved as the head and the feet. And seen from this angle, the conserved result would not have appeared anywhere as near as macabre as that which was visible when the body was uncovered.

But the decision was apparently taken and accepted. This was not the first time that a regard for aesthetics, which perhaps also covered over an unexpressed ethical concern regarding the exhibition of human remains, played a role in a decision with respect to the conservation of a prehistoric corpse.

In the next letter, written in October, Peder Nielsen gives a brief account of the practical circumstances from discovery to dispatch by rail. However, this did not constitute an archaeological finds report and no such report was ever written during those hectic days at the beginning of May. The press again got wind of the story and the headline was: 'Bog body so well preserved it is macabre!' And with respect to the missing finds report, another headline announces: 'Not a word from Silkeborg!'

Regardless of the lack of accompanying documentation sent to the National Museum, the crate containing Tollund Man was opened and a more detailed excavation and description of the find now began in earnest. This took place in the open air, in the courtyard of the National Museum's Conservation Department in Ny Vestergade. Former Keeper of National Antiquities Olaf Olsen recalls that he passed by in the yard and watched the excavation. He was struck by the fantastically well-preserved head and feet.

The person given the task of carrying out the excavation was conservator Knud Thorvildsen who, together with his archaeologist wife Elise, had been responsible for the daily running of the Borremose excavations, of which Glob was overall head. At Borremose, in 1946, 1947 and 1948, they had excavated and investigated three bog bodies. He later produced a detailed report on the

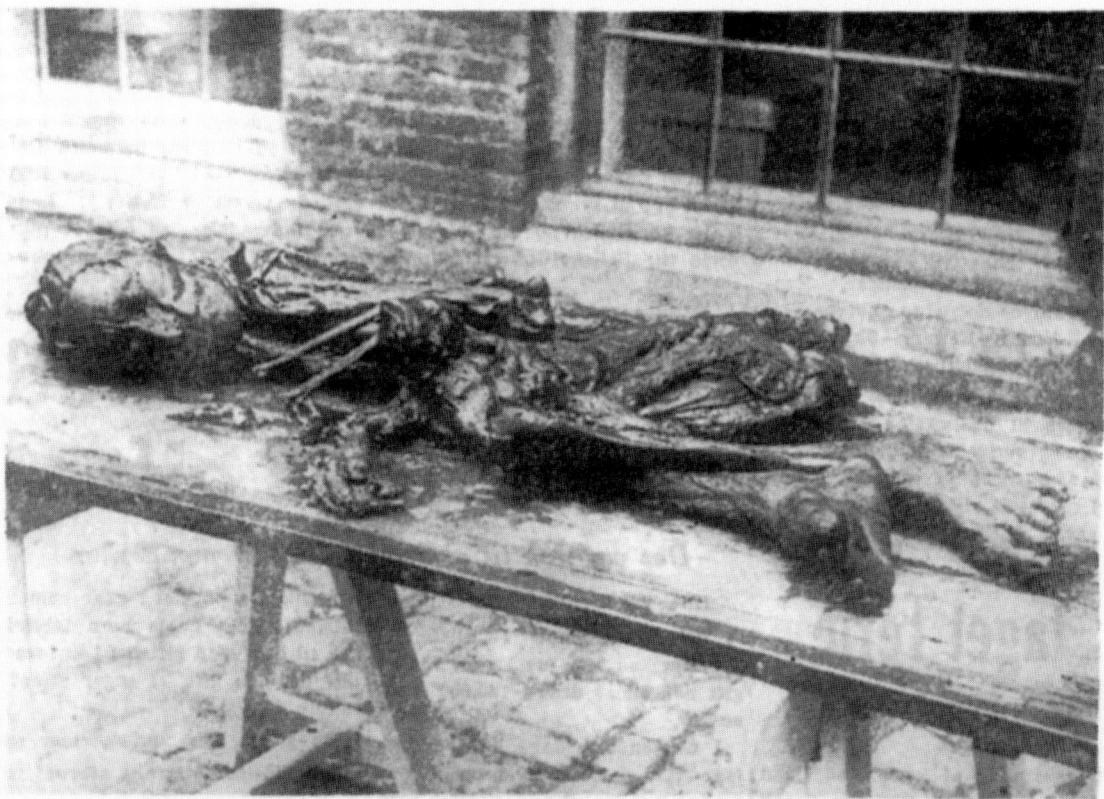

»Moselund-manden«! *Nationalmuseets ekspert, konservator Thorvildsen, har nu faaet moseliget fra Moselund ved Silkeborg »gravet ud« af den tonstunge jordblok, fundet blev sendt til København i, og her er den flere tusinde aar gamle »Moselund-mand«, der er forunderlig velbevaret. Ansigtstrækkene er ganske tydelige, ja endog mandens skægstubbe er bevaret, ligesom mandens fødder er ubeskadiget. Liget har en lædersnor stramt om halsen; men der er tvivl om, hvorvidt »Moselund-manden« i sin tid er blevet henrettet som en forbryder eller gravsat som offerlig.*

The first press photographs of the exposed Tollund Man 'confirmed' that he was a macabre sight. (Silkeborg Social-Demokrat, *27 May 1950*)

excavation and conservation of Tollund Man – a task which took more than two years to complete.

In September 1950 Knud Thorvildsen visited Funder parish where there were thirty-five scheduled barrows to be checked as part of the continued monitoring of scheduled monuments. On the same occasion a number of other archaeological localities were also visited and a small handwritten note describes Tollund Man's find site and what the finders, Viggo and Emil Højgaard, could recall when he met them there. The find site was archived in the National Museum's parish record as no. 22, Funder parish, Hids district, Viborg county.

Viggo told Thorvildsen that the discovery was made at a depth of 3.5m – the depth is given elsewhere as 2.5m, but a bog surface is far from even. He also told him that two peat spades (the T-shaped examples mentioned above) were found 3–4m from the corpse and that they, too, lay at the base of the bog.

On the same occasion, the brothers also mentioned the discovery of another corpse (Elling Woman), made about a decade earlier, providing the surprising

Close-up of the newly excavated head. *(Photo: Lennart Larsen)*

The peat spade which lay next to Tollund Man made the newspaper, but not the museum
– it disappeared.

additional information that this body was found together with a wooden paddle.
Viggo and Emil did not, however, know what had happened to the body and said
that the finders were either dead or had moved away (the body was in fact taken to
the National Museum in 1938).

Finds of several double-ended wooden paddles have been recorded from bogs
in Jutland. Their function was initially difficult to interpret but then Danish
researchers discovered that identical implements are used today in Papua New
Guinea and that they were not intended for paddling a boat but were actually
digging implements. Any idea of a direct connection between this, the world's
most faraway place, and Jutland is of course absurd. Instead it suggests that it
is perfectly possible that two specialised inventions can arise independent of
place, time and cultural sphere. It therefore provides food for thought for those
academics who attempt to demonstrate emigration and immigration routes with
the aid of finds of specialised implements which they claim 'prove' that the same
people were responsible.

Iron Age tools for cutting peat: the T-shaped spade and the spade in the form of a double paddle. *(Photo: Silkeborg Museum)*

The Danish 'paddles', i.e. double spades, have been radiocarbon dated to the Early Iron Age. Research carried out at Lejre Land of Legends (formerly Lejre Historical-Archaeological Experimental Centre) has demonstrated that they are well-suited to digging in peat. When one end has become worn in the course of digging, the implement is simply turned through 180 degrees and digging continues until that end is also worn. By that time it is 'probably lunchtime', as I was told by one of the researchers working on these implements – ethnologist Professor Axel Steensberg.

THE EXCAVATION

On returning home from his monument monitoring duties, which were scheduled for the outdoor season, Knud Thorvildsen's detailed investigations of Tollund Man continued. These had the character of an excavation that could have taken place at the find site but which now unfolded under much more satisfactory circumstances. Fine instruments could be put to use and it was possible to keep the peat block and its contents wet during the entire excavation process. A fungicide, probably formalin, must also have been employed. The National Museum's photographer Lennart Larsen kept a regular photographic record of the appearance of the corpse before conservation and/or desiccation perhaps brought about changes.

As is true of more or less all archaeological investigations, a description was made layer by layer from the top downwards as the find was uncovered.

After removing the peat which had been laid around to protect the body, Knud Thorvildsen was able to note that the corpse lay in a reddish layer of fibrous sphagnum peat. Peat cutters refer to this as 'dog flesh' because it is of poor quality as fuel. The peat over the body, apart from that which adhered to it, appeared to have been disturbed. This most probably happened when the extent of the body was being established, as it was necessary to determine the size of the crate required for transport. The archaeologists had also been rather 'unprofessional' in their behaviour out in the bog as they had disturbed the peat in order to catch a glimpse of the bog body's face.

The layers under the body appeared untouched. Directly beneath it there was a thin 2–5cm thick layer of 'dog flesh', which rested on a dark, markedly sandy layer in which no plant remains were visible. This sequence suggests that Tollund Man had been deposited in a peat cutting which had already stood open for a short time.

The corpse lay on its right side with legs drawn up and arms flexed in front. Apart from a leather cap on the head and a leather belt about the waist, the body was naked and the skin bore no further marks. A leather rope was tight about his neck.

The head was exceptionally well preserved. The hair was cut short, 2–3cm in length, with no styling, and the eyebrows were partially preserved. There was also very short stubble on the upper lip, chin and cheeks. It is a common belief that hair and nails continue to grow after death, but the truth is that desiccation, together with the absence of blood pressure 'filling out' the skin, makes the stubble and nails appear longer. The eyes were closed, as was the mouth with its well-preserved lips. The face was relaxed – like someone asleep.

The upper torso was slightly bent forwards and had most of its skin preserved intact. The left side of the chest and the shoulder did, however, show some degree of decay as the epidermis was missing over large areas. The right side of the body was well-preserved, although the shoulder and the lowermost ribs protruded through the skin. Along the back a sharp cut could be seen, clearly caused by a spade thrust from a peat digger. The hip socket protruded through the skin on the left side. The abdomen lay in folds and the genitalia were well preserved and male.

The left upper arm lay alongside the chest, with the lower arm pointed upwards at a sharp angle; the hand lay about 10cm from the face. Only the upper arm was preserved with skin intact; the lower arm and hand appeared merely as bones. The finger bones had been disarticulated during recovery from the bog. A couple of them had been placed on top of the corpse when it was sent to the museum. The right upper arm lay alongside the chest; the lower arm lay almost at right angles to the upper arm with the hand bent slightly downwards only about 10cm from the left knee. The upper arm was well preserved, whereas the lower arm was partially skeletonised, as was the hand with only the thumb with its nail completely preserved.

The right knee and thigh lay close to the abdomen, the lower leg lay in direct continuation of the body with the foot was bent slightly downwards. The thigh was well preserved, although the skeletal end at the knee had been broken off and was turned through 90 degrees. The tibia was almost completely exposed, but the flesh of the calf, around the fibula, was well preserved, although slightly decomposed. The foot was exceptionally well preserved, but the toes lacked nails. The left thigh extended almost at a right angle out from the body; the lower leg was bent backwards such that the tibia rested on the right leg about 12cm above the ankle. The epidermis of the thigh was somewhat decomposed and the upper part had been cut through in the bog in the course of its discovery – probably the event which caused Emil to hesitate a moment, resulting in the find being recognised as a body. The patella was loose but still in situ. The tibia was completely skeletonised. In contrast, the fibula was almost completely flesh- and skin-covered. The foot was well preserved although without nails on the toes.

A couple of further comments can be added to Thorvildsen's description. For example, the important piece of information that no marks were found on the

Opposite: The left side – the one which was uppermost in the bog – exposed at the National Museum. *(Photo: Lennart Larsen)*

body which could be interpreted as traces left by clothes that had decayed completely during the body's time in the bog – clothes made of, for example, linen or nettle fibre.

An actual height measurement was not carried out due the curled-up state of the body. However, by measuring from the top of the head to the hip, from here to the knee, then continuing down the lower surface to the heel, the height can be estimated as about 161cm. Whether this corresponds to his height in life is uncertain as most bodies tend to shrink with time in the bog. However, if this was Tollund Man's height then it matches the average height of the world's population today.

The description also reveals how random preservation in the bog had been – the right hand was skeletonised apart from the thumb. This, in turn, was so well preserved that the police were subsequently able to examine the fingerprint.

THE LEATHER CAP

The hair on the corpse's head, dyed red by the bog water, was covered by a sewn leather cap. Its top was somewhat damaged, probably by the thrust of a peat spade in the bog. The cap was secured to the head with two thin leather straps attached by small loops which, when the cap was in position on the corpse, were located at the temples. The straps were drawn tight about the head just in front of the ears and had cut furrows into the cheeks. A bow tied at the right temple, hidden under the hat, joined the straps together. The cap was sewn as a tuque and was turned so that the hair side of the hide faced inwards. The skin appeared to be that of a sheep. The cap was sewn up inside out and then turned the right way out again to be worn. This is clearly evident as the outermost 2cm of the cap tip has not been pressed out after being sewn. The cap was made from eight pieces of leather, joined to form three encircling parts. In appearance and date it is reminiscent of the headwear found on a bog body from Søgårds Mose. The latter was, however, only made from two pieces of sheepskin. Yet another cap, found with a bog body from Rønbjerg near Skive, was also said to have been similar but has not been preserved.

Opposite: Tollund Man has been turned over and lies on a cloth laid out by the excavators. *(Photo: Lennart Larsen)*

THE BELT

The belt positioned around his hips lay in folds behind his back, but tight against his abdomen. It was tied at the left side and measured 77.5cm in circumference. It was made of thin, hairless leather and had been unevenly cut, being 1.9–2.4cm in width. It was though 3.5cm wide at the end equipped with an 'eye' or slit through which the other end, only 1.3cm in width, had been threaded and bound with a loop knot which could be loosened by a slight tug on the 14cm length which hang loose.

THE ROPE AROUND THE NECK

A leather rope or cord sat tightly around the neck. A knot had been tied at one end forming a long 'eye' around 6cm in length and the other end of the cord had been threaded through this. The 'running noose' which resulted was placed around the neck so that the knot of the 'eye' lay on the left side with the 'eye' facing to the rear; the noose was tightened at the back of the neck.

The free end of the cord lay in a tangle over the left side of the body, running over the shoulder, beneath and along the right side of the torso, ending directly in front of the right hip. The free end here at the hip had been cut neatly and squarely, whereas the other end at the neck terminated in a simple knot. When the cord was removed from the neck it was evident that it had made distinct furrows in the skin at the sides and under the chin, whereas no marks had been produced at the back of the neck where the noose was located. The cord had been braided from two strips of leather about 2cm wide and its length, from the cut-off end to the outer limit of the 'eye', was 155cm. The distance enclosed by the noose, i.e. the circumference of the neck, was 25cm.

In addition to this information, Knud Thorvildsen records in his report that, during the exposure and removal of the body at the Conservation Department, no finds or observations were made of any kind over and above those described. He emphasises that no evidence of mutilation of the body were found apart from that revealed by the cord around the neck.

As the body was being excavated, pollen samples were taken from the peat deposits around and beneath it. These samples could potentially provide information on the landscape and the pollen zone – or climatic period – to which the body belongs. However, this method is dependent on the pollen being deposited undisturbed and at the same time as the object or the body from which the sample is taken.

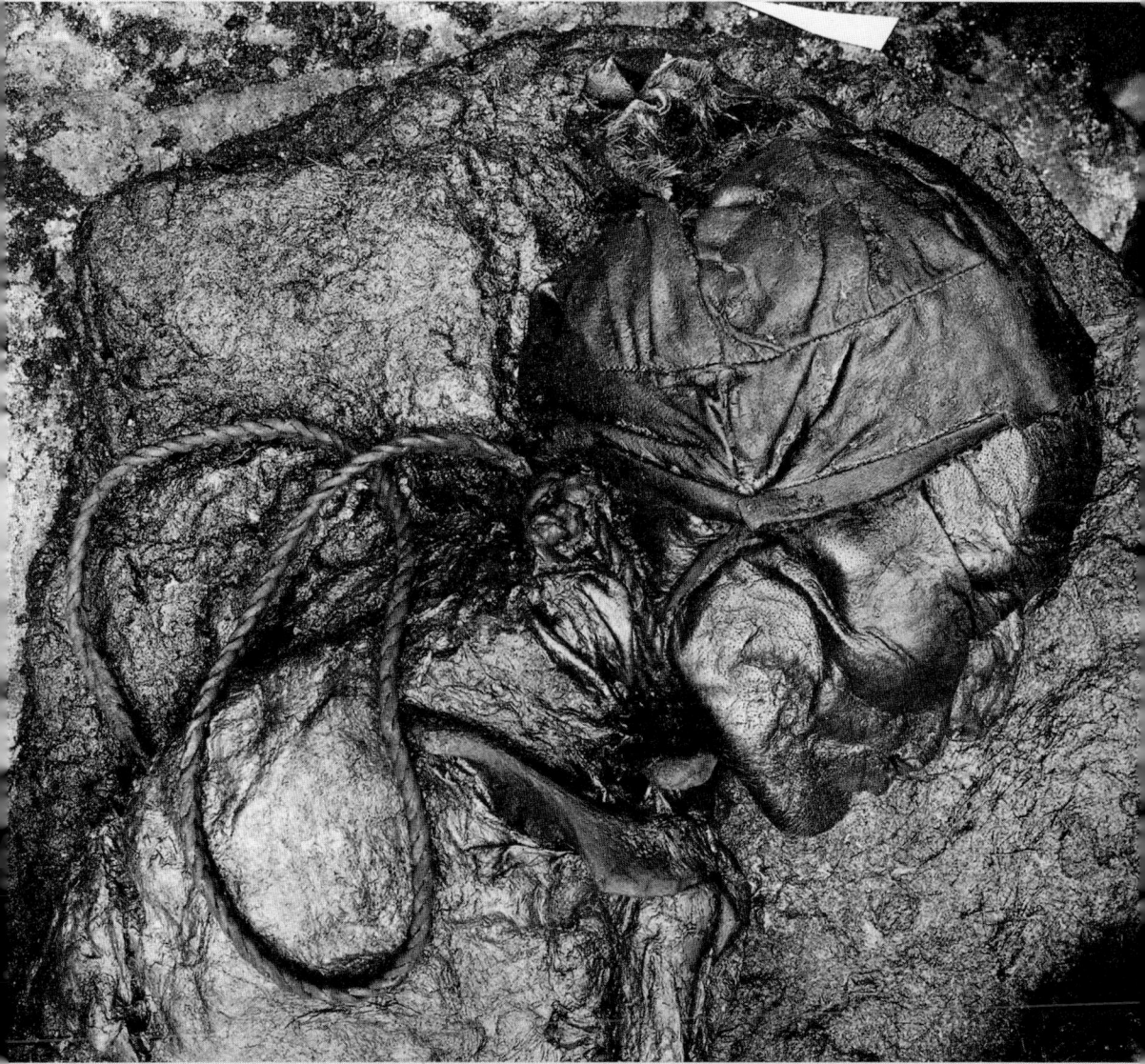

A leather cord with a running noose sat tightly around his neck. *(Photo: Lennart Larsen)*

These pollen samples were submitted to Moselaboratoriet (the Bog Laboratory), as it was then known, at the National Museum with the relevant information. A preliminary analysis of the samples, carried out by Børge Brorson Christensen, simply revealed that the body had been placed in the bog at some point after the Neolithic period. Two years later, a minor palaeoecological investigation was carried out at the find site.

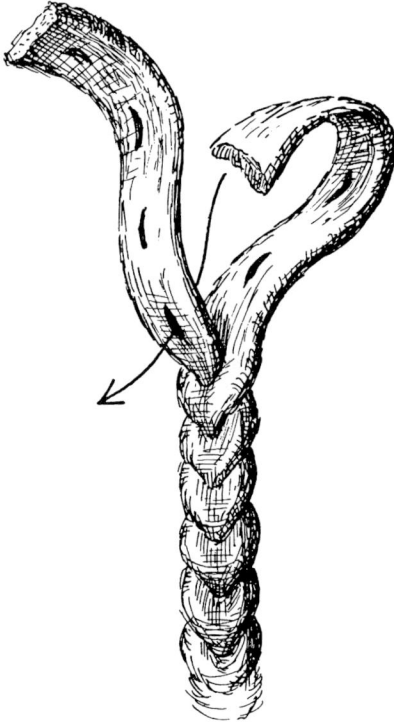

The rope had been braided together
from two thin strips of leather.
(Drawing: Knud Thorvildsen)

After the body had been comprehensively photographed following complete excavation at the National Museum, it was transported to Bispebjerg Hospital on the morning of 31 May and handed over to consultant physician Christian Bastrup. The head and the upper part of the torso were x-rayed; probably the first time that this technique was applied to an archaeological find in Denmark.

Due to advanced decalcification of the bones, the image of the neck vertebrae was not very clear, but Dr Bastrup did not believe that these vertebrae were damaged. The image also revealed that the brain was remarkably well preserved, although much shrunken.

Pathologist Kay Schourup also examined the body and concluded that the cord, as it was positioned around the neck of the corpse, was unlikely to have been used for strangulation. Instead, hanging was the most obvious explanation for the position of the cord. The fact that the neck vertebrae appeared undamaged was not necessarily significant as vertebral injury was not always caused during hanging.

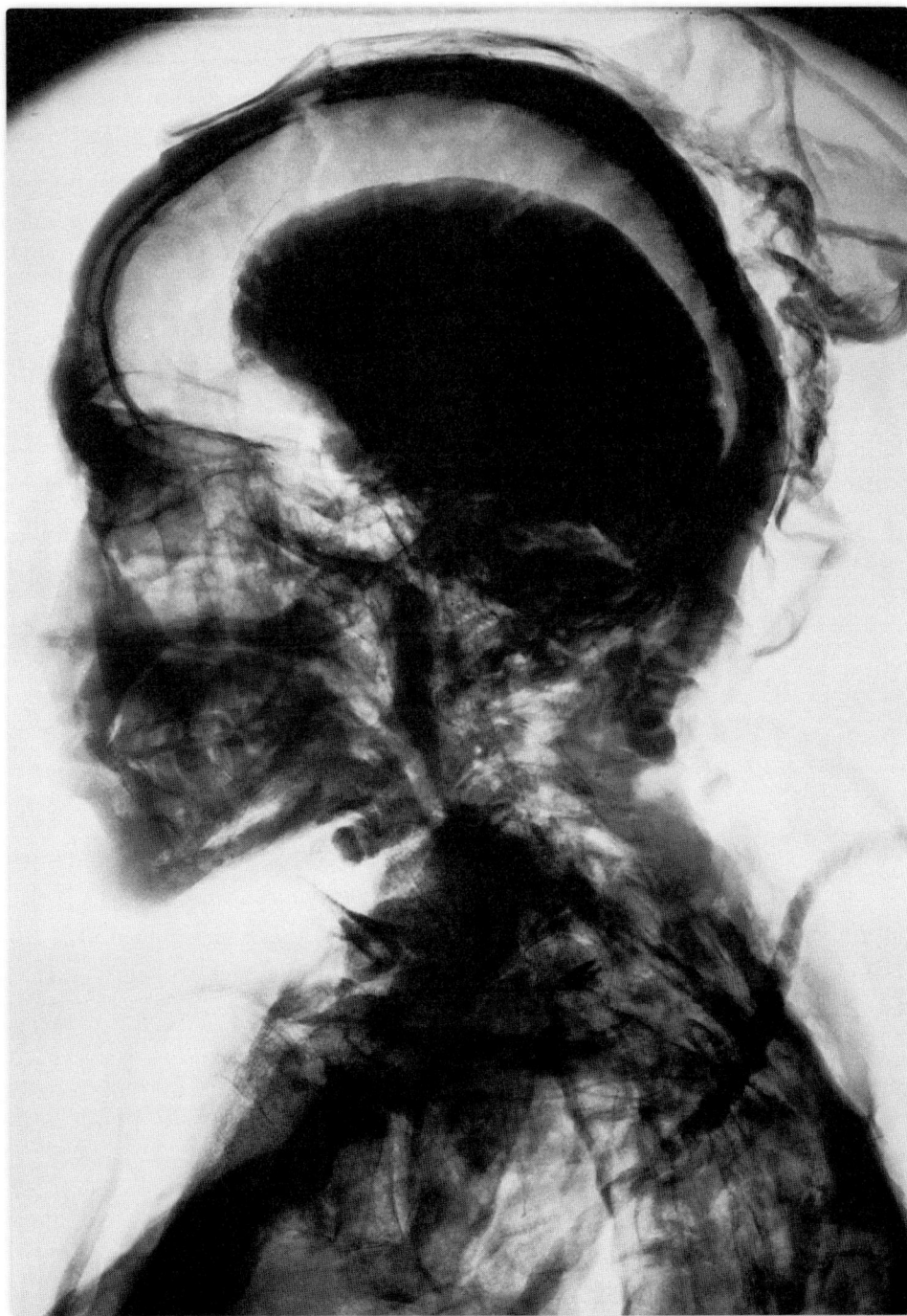

X-ray of Tollund Man's head. *(Photo: Bispebjerg Hospital)*

THE LAST MEAL

The x-ray images revealed Tollund Man's internal organs to be partially intact and the doctors involved in the detailed examinations in 1950 were tempted to make use of the opportunity to investigate how the viscera had resisted the influence of the acidic bog water and whether there were traces of possible illness. Last, but not least, they wanted to discover what the content of the corpse's gut could reveal about diet in the Early Iron Age.

The post-mortem examination, led by Dr Bjovulf Vimtrup, prosector at Bispebjerg Hospital, proved that Tollund Man's interior were just as well preserved as his exterior, although the viscera had lost their original volume and had, due to the pressure of the peat, become flattened. Even so, the physicians were able to identify each individual organ and locate the alimentary canal without difficulty.

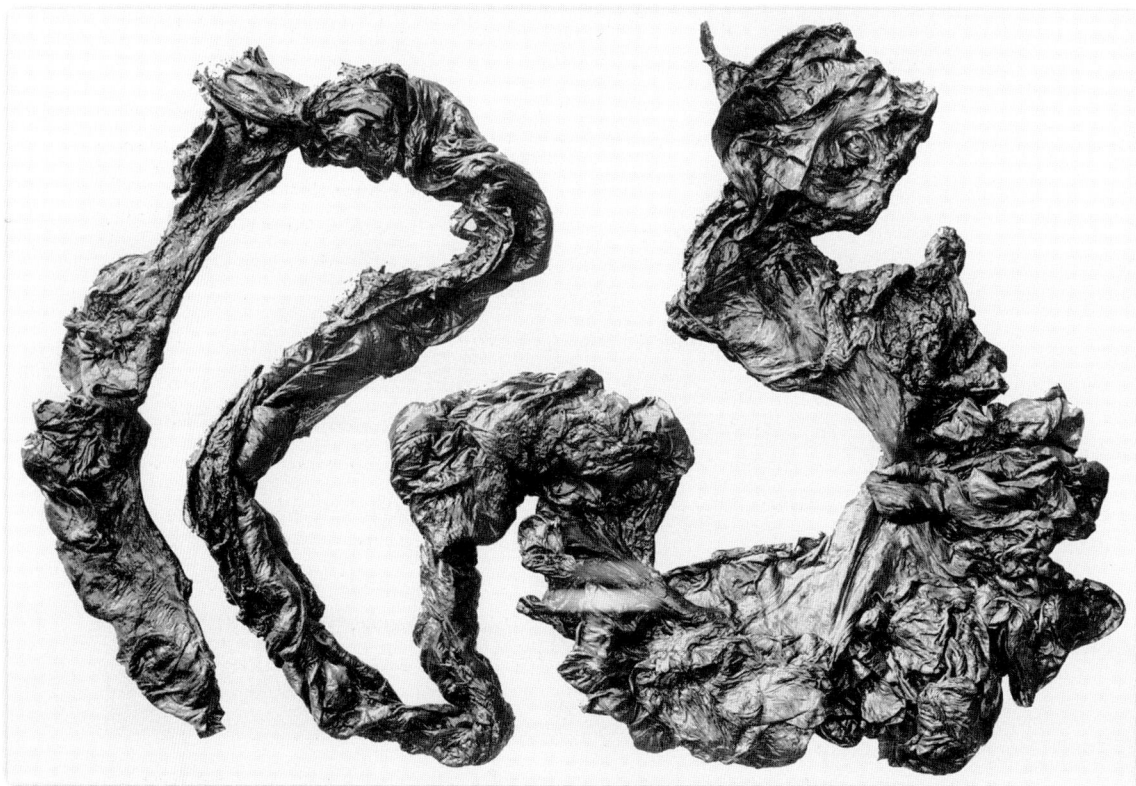

Tollund Man's large intestine which contained most of the remains of his last meal. *(Photo: The National Museum)*

The latter was removed in one intact piece extending from the stomach to the anus and sent for analysis to a botanist expert in identifying seeds and other plant remains – even when they had been slightly degraded by digestion. A similar investigation had already been carried out in 1946, when the contents of the large intestine from a bog body found in Borremose were examined by botanist Inger Brandt.

It was botanist Hans Helbæk who was responsible for the investigation of Tollund Man's gut contents. The stomach and the small intestine contained only a few food remains, whereas the main body of material was found in the large intestine, consistent with him having eaten twelve to twenty-four hours before he was hanged.

It was not possible to give the precise composition of the meal as the resistance of various plant remains to the digestive processes varies. However, Hans Helbæk's investigations, and a minor supplementary investigation carried out in 2003, revealed that the food eaten by Tollund Man must have been in the form of porridge or gruel. This was apparently made using bog water as some fresh leaves of bog moss (sphagnum) had 'found their way' into the meal; they may though also have been in the water he drank.

Helbæk reached the conclusion that the main component of the gruel or porridge was barley, with linseed providing the fat content. Linseed is prescribed today as a laxative; however, if taken over a longer period, this effect declines. Oats were also included in the gruel. These three are all cultivated crop plants. Added to them were the ground-up seeds of weed plants – some in quantities which revealed that they had been gathered. Others must be seen as random contamination when the Iron Age field was harvested; these fields were notoriously weedy. The weed seeds which had been deliberately gathered were those of persicaria, fat hen, corn spurrey, gold of pleasure, field pansy and possibly hemp nettle. The more coincidental species were barnyard grass, curled dock, sheep sorrel, chickweed, pennycress, shepherd's purse, wallflower, navew and plantain. The extent to which the various species were included as 'bulk' or as 'flavourings' is of course uncertain today. A meal closely corresponding to that eaten by another famous bog body, Grauballe Man, has on numerous occasions been reconstructed and eaten – with pleasure by some, whereas others believe that it was to disguise this taste that the Danes invented aquavit!

An important detail is that there were no traces of either meat or fresh fruit in the gut contents. The meal was probably prepared from the stored supplies of summer crops. This is consistent with the winter deposition of Tollund Man and the other well-preserved bog bodies. This is the dark time of the year – the time when bog water is so cold that nature's conservation processes can do full justice. Iron Age inhumation graves dated to just after AD 1 tell us that the food placed in the graves for the journey to the Kingdom of the Dead usually included parts of animals, i.e. joints of meat!

As was the case with other bog bodies which have been investigated, Tollund Man was found to be infected with the intestinal parasite whipworm.

DISMEMBERMENT OF THE CORPSE

Knud Thorvildsen describes what happened next:

> Following examination, Dr Vimtrup severed the corpse's head from the body because, after careful consideration, it had been decided that only the head should be conserved. This decision was made by Dr Therkel Mathiassen who accepted that the find, on completion of conservation, should be handed over to Silkeborg Museum which was responsible for its submission.

Whereas the dismembered body was simply stored and, with time, allowed to shrink and become hugely deformed, the head began a process of conservation.

The decision to dismember the remainder of the corpse now seems obviously wrong. The account given does not perhaps directly identify the person who made the decision, but a letter from Therkel Mathiassen to Silkeborg Museum more than suggests that the decision was his.

Moreover, the fact that the dismembered corpse was simply allowed to shrink and become deformed also seems extremely peculiar. At that time – and it is still the case today – one of the bog bodies from Borremose was kept stored in formalin in the National Museum's cellar. The rationale was that this rendered it possible to carry out further investigations and have the opportunity to apply new methods of conservation in the future. For many years, it formed part of the 'initiation rites' for newly-appointed student assistants at the National Museum to peer down on the bog body as it lay in a bath of formalin solution in the museum's dark cellar. Why was the same not done for Tollund Man?

Moselundmanden i alvorlig fare?

Hans hoved er henlagt i en kasserolle paa Nationalmuseet!

Der er stadig intet nyt om præpareringen af det moselig, der i sommer blev fundet ved Moselund, og som skulle være sikret Silkeborg museum, saafremt konservering var muligt. Overbibliotekar Peder N i e l s e n har netop i dag fra Nationalmuseet faaet oplyst, at man faktisk ikke ved, hvad der skal gøres ved moseliget, eller rettere, hvad der k a n gøres ved det!

PRÆPARERING AF FØDDER OG HOVED?

I den tid, konservator T h o r v i l d s e n har arbejdet med fundet, har „Moselundmanden« adskillige gange haft besøg fra Silkeborg, og det er ikke særligt opmuntrende bulletiner, der er bragt med hjem. Mens videnskabsmændene har dissekeret det meste af „Moselundmanden«, bl. a. for at undersøge, hvad hans sidste maaltid har bestaaet af, er konservatorer gaaet i gang med at forsøge en tørpræparering af moseligets meget velbevarede fødder. Man ved endnu ikke, om det lykkes at rekonstruere og bevare liget i samme intakte stand, som det blev fundet; man ved end ikke, om det lykkes at tørpræparere fødderne, og indtil videre opbevares ligets hoved i en kasserolle med vædske!

Der er stadig mulighed for at sikre fundet ved at opbevare det i vædske, men i saa fald vil det ikke blive den tilgængelige museumsattraktion, man havde haabet. Ifald det ikke lykkes at bevare fundet i sin oprindelige skikkelse, staar haabet til, at hovedet med den usædvanlige læderhat og rebstykket om halsen kan sikres uforgængelighed.

DET GAAR SMAAT MED MUSEET

Ikke mindst i forbindelse med dette fund har spørgsmaalet om Silkeborg museum været drøftet. En del af Silkeborg Hovedgaard er som bekendt stillet til Museumsforeningens raadighed, og der er forlængst gjort forberedelser til bygningens indretning. Det gaar dog meget smaat med dette arbejde. Man har faaet parketstave hjem til gulvet, men arbejdet er foreløbig sinket paa grund af haandværkernes travlhed.

h r.

'Moselundmanden i alvorlig fare?' (Moselund Man in danger?), was the headline run by Central Jutland newspapers who were following work at the National Museum from a distance. *(Silkeborg Social-Demokrat, 4 October 1950)*

CONSERVATION

The conservation of the head was a long, drawn-out process which, in basic terms, involved replacing the preservative bog water in the cells with a stable solid substance. If allowed to dry out, the head would shrink like the body and become deformed – undergoing exactly the same process as can be observed when a bouquet of cut flowers is left somewhere dry for any period of time.

Knud Thorvildsen and Børge Brorson Christensen were responsible for the conservation process. The method had not previously been tried and tested on human material of this size so it was very much experimental. In a lecture given by Brorson Christensen to the Prehistoric Society in London in 1972, he said that the inspiration for the treatment came from the preparation of

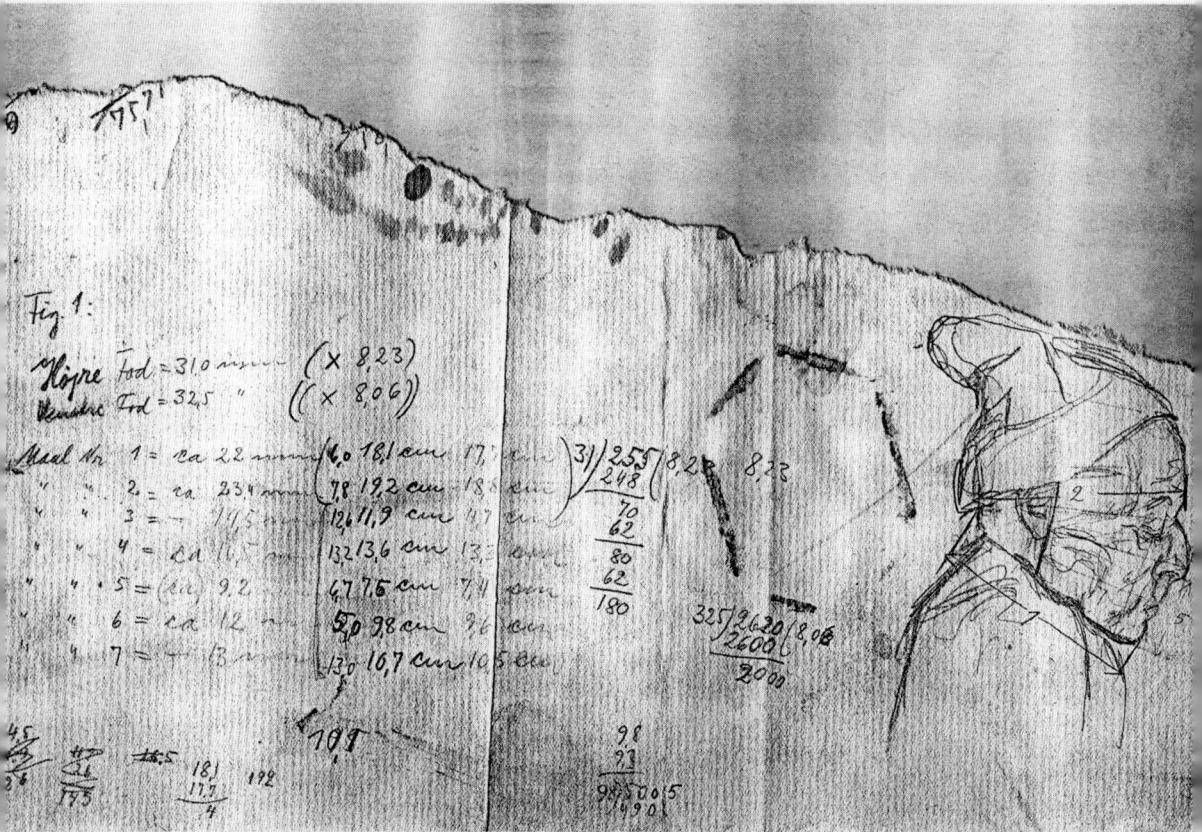

Knud Thorvildsen, who was the excavator at the National Museum, carefully measured Tollund Man's head before and after conservation. *(Drawing: Knud Thorvildsen)*

biological material for microscopic examination; this involves paraffin wax and dehydrating solutions.

The head was first left for six months in water to which formalin and acetic acid had been added in order for this anti-bacterial fluid to replace the bog water. Shortly before Christmas the formalin/acetic acid solution was replaced with 30 per cent alcohol. At monthly intervals the immersion fluid was then changed to a steadily higher alcohol concentration until, by midsummer in 1951, the head was transferred to 99 per cent alcohol. The solvent toluol was then added to the alcohol and, on 15 August, the alcohol-toluol mixture was replaced with pure toluol. The aim of this extended process was to replace the bog water with fluids which could be mixed without 'curdling'. The final fluid had to be able to dissolve wax – carnauba wax, to which a little beeswax had been added. This readily becomes liquid on heating but would be solid and durable at the temperatures at which the head was subsequently to be exhibited.

The citizens of Silkeborg had the opportunity, via the press, to follow the conservation process and no great optimism was expressed: 'Moselund Man at serious risk?' read one newspaper headline, followed by the subtitle, 'His head placed in a saucepan at the National Museum'.

During the final wax treatment the head was placed in an oven and on the year's shortest day the temperature was reduced to 78° Celsius and the wax mixture was poured off. The head was then allowed to cool in the air and was doused with cold water.

In February, the conservation process was considered complete. The head appeared unchanged, both with respect to its relative proportions and its facial features. Nevertheless, Thorvildsen's very detailed measurements, taken before and after conservation, revealed that it had shrunk by about 12 per cent. Subsequent experiments have demonstrated that the main cause of shrinkage is that wax decreases in volume when cooled.

It was decided that the right side of Tollund Man's head, the side which had faced downwards in the bog, should now face upwards when exhibited – a minor bevelling at the neck supported this new position.

No mention is made in the report of the fact that the well-preserved right thumb and foot were kept in a preservative fluid, probably alcohol. In 1970, they were conserved using polyethylene glycol (PEG), followed by freeze drying. In both cases the conservation was initially a success, but later there were problems of flaking with the foot – a process which unfortunately is unlikely to be stoppable.

The leather cap, the leather belt and the cord from around the neck were conserved shortly after their recovery using a lanolin mixture which was the traditional method at that time. Subsequent checks have revealed that this approach was excellent as the objects have remained stable ever since.

After a brief exhibition in the vestibule of the National Museum at the beginning of June 1952, Tollund Man was then, according to Thorvildsen, handed over to Silkeborg Museum.

This statement is, however, only partially true as it only applied to the head. For many years it was not known what had happened to the other, now desiccated, parts of Tollund Man's body.

3

THE BOG AS A TREASURE CHEST

T he Højgaard family were initially in some doubt as to whether the corpse they had found was prehistoric or the result of a recent criminal act. For them, and for many others, it was simply incredible that human bodies could be preserved in bogs for millennia. When, in 1942, a bog body was found in Bredmose near Arden in Himmerland, the police called to the scene were in no doubt – it was obvious that this individual was not on any missing persons list. But to keep the record straight it was recommended that the corpse be reburied in a nearby churchyard. It was only through the intervention of a local museum official from Aalborg that the body was correctly recorded as a prehistoric find.

There is no common denominator in how people have ended up in bogs. Temporally, there is too great a difference between a prehistoric Nordic bog body and the victim of a modern Irish civil war, both of whom have ended up in similar surroundings. Moreover, bog bodies have been recorded from places as diverse as Russia and the Florida swamps.

In the past, researchers have attempted to find a single factor linking bodies found in bogs; some even continue to do so. In my opinion, this research produces results which are just as lacking in perspective as the squaring of the circle.

For a corpse to become a bog body requires both very special natural conditions and active human intervention. The people who placed a corpse in a bog were, in all probability, totally unaware that their actions were contributing to the preservation of this corpse for many years, millennia even.

Many other bodies – very probably the majority – were placed in bogs without the necessary preserving conditions being in attendance. These bodies decayed long ago and have entered into nature's great cycle, although if there were

The landscape at Bølling Lake – a mixture of open water and various types of bog. *(Photo: Silkeborg Museum)*

appropriate conditions for the preservation of bone, the corpse could potentially be found later as a skeleton.

If we want to find an explanation for the natural conditions necessary for the preservation of intact corpses with bones, skin and hair, we can very appropriately turn to the discovery of Tollund Man in Bjældskovdal.

The valley of Bjældskovdal forms part of the great Bølling Lake complex which covers a total area of 350ha and is very precisely located on the Jutland watershed. The latter is such a literal phenomenon that the lake's two outlets, the rivers Funder Å and Skygge Å, have their sources at the opposite ends of the lake and flow in different directions. Funder Å runs into the River Gudenå – flowing past Silkeborg and Randers before becoming a part of Randers Fjord and then emptying into the Kattegat. Skygge Å, which is known downstream as Karup Å and ultimately Skive Å, passes the town of Karup before, just outside Skive, emptying into Skive Fjord, which is part of the Limfjord. In theory, a fish can take a short cut from Randers to Skive by way of Bølling Lake.

Since the retreat of the ice about 13,000 years ago, Bølling Lake has constituted a very large area of shallow water which represented an Eldorado for fish and game. Consequently, it was very attractive to people – first hunters and gatherers and later farmers who supplemented their crops with fish and game.

This shallow lake, and the valleys which surround it, hosts many different landscape forms – a natural 'mixed bag' of habitats – from open water and reed bed to extensive areas of peat bog. These bogs can be lowland bogs with natural meadows, flush bogs where springs break the surface, and raised bogs. There is also a wealth of transitional forms from one landscape type to the other.

A constant determining factor for the extent of the lake and the size of the bogs has been climate. This shifted from the warmth of the Neolithic and Bronze Age to the wetness of the Iron Age and the cold of the Middle Ages. Until about 150 years ago it was almost totally free of human influence. Today, human intervention in the form of climate change and nitrogen emissions appears to have had major consequences for the life of the lake and the bogs around it. The release of nutritive salts, both water- and airborne, has promoted a level of tree growth which can only be kept at bay with a chainsaw.

The greatest influence on Bølling Lake has been modern human exploitation of the lake and its surroundings. Peat has been cut and marl has been quarried to such an extent that only minor areas remain untouched.

The natural and cultural history of the lake's first millennia can be read by palaeoecologists and archaeologists from its deep deposits of peat and mud. Pollen produced by plants has a remarkable ability to survive when, scattered by the wind, it falls on the surface of a bog or sinks to the bottom of a calm lake. Thousands of years later, scientists can extract these pollen grains and, with the aid of a microscope, identify and count them, as the pollen of every tree and herb has its own distinct morphology. If a pollen sample is taken in contact with an archaeological artefact found by an archaeologist in bog or lake sediments, it is possible to discover the characteristic nature of the surrounding vegetation at the time the object was in use. By comparison with a general pollen reference framework – a so-called pollen diagram – built up for the history of the local vegetation, this spectrum can then be 'matched' and reveal a date for when the object was deposited in the bog.

Pollen is deposited year after year and is preserved in sediments as they accumulate at the bottom of lakes and in peat bogs. Peat accumulates at an average rate of 2–3mm per year. In Denmark, the pollen data reveals a landscape which at first was very open. Then, around 11,000 years ago, birch and pine trees appeared and by about 8,500 years ago they had been joined by lime and most of the forest's other deciduous trees: oak, elm, hazel and alder. A few millennia later, the first traces of pollen from the crops of Neolithic farmers turned up and the forest picture changed: the sharp flint axes of the Neolithic farmers felled the primeval forest in Denmark – forever!

Oak pollen is also found in much later deposits, for example from the Bronze Age. Here, however, pollen analysts need not search for the pollen with their microscopes – instead they can examine the great coffins of hollowed-out oak trunks in which Bronze Age people were buried beneath mighty barrows; Egtved Girl is probably the best known example. Dendrochronology or tree-ring dating – one of archaeology's most powerful dating methods – was applied to her oak coffin in order to discover the year in which she was buried: 1370 BC.

One of the greatest human interventions in the life of the lake is the 'nature rehabilitation' project launched in recent years and aimed at restoring the lake to how it is thought once to have been. Precisely when 'once' was is very much a modern human decision. Should it recreate the situation immediately after the Ice Age? Or that of the Neolithic, or the Iron Age, or just before the major draining of the lake at the end of the nineteenth century? Back then, Hedeselskabet (the Danish Land Development Service) developed a model for the cultivation of large natural areas which were 'unproductive'. This took place under the motto 'Hvad udad tabes skal indad vindes' ('Outward loss, inward gain') as a reaction to the surrender of Southern Jutland following the terrible military defeat to Germany suffered by Denmark in 1864.

Bølling Lake encapsulated a dramatic history of Denmark for those able to read it. With the continued drying out and cultivation of the lake bed and the bogs along its shores, increasing numbers of finds saw the light of day. Field implements cut deeper and the peat crumbled so the protective layer over the archaeological remains became thinner and thinner. Many Stone Age settlements, dating back to the very earliest Mesolithic, suddenly appeared as did carved amber animals, presumably depicting the beasts a Stone Age hunter hoped to meet – a custom revived in the Iron Age – alongside parts of a Y-shaped cart shaft dating from the end of the Neolithic. A long sequence of stepping stones then appeared which had once enabled Iron Age people to travel from shore to shore without getting their feet wet – more or less. And numerous wooden spades from prehistoric peat cutting, both those with short transverse handles and those shaped like 'paddles'. Finally came the bog bodies.

Flint and stone tools can survive everywhere, whereas implements and other objects of wood, bone and antler make greater demands on the conserving properties of the soil – constant wetness is a minimum requirement. Furthermore, if skin, hair and leather are to be preserved for millennia then a raised bog, with its special physical and chemical composition, is the only option. There were several raised bogs along the shores of Bølling Lake and in the valleys surrounding it. Bjældskovdal was one of these, and the bog bodies found there – for there are more than just Tollund Man – demonstrate the very special conserving properties they possess. In Denmark this type of bog is most common in Jutland, but it is also found elsewhere in north-west Europe, especially in oceanic coastal areas.

During the excavation of Tollund Man, Børge Brorson Christensen, who was also a pollen analyst, took samples of the peat adhering to the body. His analyses revealed that the peat probably dated from the Neolithic. However, as the body had been buried in a pit cut down through overlying peat layers, his results did not provide a date of the body but only showed that it must be later than the Neolithic. Only by comparing pollen samples from Tollund Man with samples taken as close as possible to the actual find spot would it be possible to arrive at a description of the pollen zone (or climatic period) from which the body originated. Before the radiocarbon dating method of the atomic age, pollen analysis was considered the best way of determining the age of a find.

It was well known that there was some uncertainty associated with pollen dating but it could scarcely have been imagined that, with the advent of the radiocarbon method of absolute dating, the introduction of agriculture to Denmark would suddenly be shifted 1,000 years back in time. Instead of the pollen-analytical date of 3000 BC, the introduction of farming now had an absolute date of 4000 BC.

Over the course of ten November days in 1952, scientists from the National Museum's Bog Laboratory undertook a detailed palaeoecological study of Tollund

Man's find site. The laboratory had originally been established to deal with the many finds which turned up as a consequence of peat extraction during the Second World War and the post-war period. It was the head of the laboratory, Jørgen Troels-Smith, and another member of staff, Svend Jørgensen, who were responsible for the investigation, which they considered preliminary. Troels-Smith subsequently wrote the following to Silkeborg Museum:

> As you are probably already aware, museum curator Svend Jørgensen and I have recently had the opportunity to investigate the find site for Tollund Man in Bjelskovdal. A 20m long peat baulk still stands, located 10–15m east of the find site; in this peat baulk we have identified two old peat cuttings, both of which are filled up with later Sphagnum peat. According to the samples which were taken from Tollund Man at the National Museum, together with the circumstances in the bog, we consider it reasonable to conclude that Tollund Man was placed in an old peat cutting. The age of the peat cutting – and thereby also of Tollund Man – will hopefully become apparent from the pollen analytical investigations which will, however, probably take a longer period of time as the task is very complex. You see, it awakened our curiosity when we were told by Emil Højgaard that on the day before the discovery of Tollund Man a wooden peat spade was found about 3m away and the depth at which it was found was about the same as that for Tollund Man. Later, at a somewhat greater distance from the find site, a further similar peat spade was found, also of wood; however this is no longer in existence. Precisely because we believe there was an old peat cutting at the spot are we naturally very interested in having the opportunity to look more closely at the peat spade which is kept at Silkeborg Museum and we would therefore be very grateful if you would send it to the undersigned. As soon as we have had the opportunity to examine it and identify the wood, it will be returned.

Rather shame-faced, Silkeborg Museum replied that the aforementioned wooden spade found near Tollund Man had been lost and that this happened while stationmaster Holger Hansen was in the process of its conservation. The reason was that the museum was still in a state of chaos as a consequence of moving premises. Fortunately, the spade was relocated, duly recorded and sent to the National Museum.

Back at the National Museum, a letter was sent from the Bog Laboratory to the museum's Prehistoric Department which was responsible for archaeological excavations, stating that:

Curator at the National Museum Svend Jørgensen standing on top of the peat baulk which shows evidence of peat cutting in the Iron Age. *(Photo: J. Troels-Smith)*

A section located a few metres from the find site was examined and a single series of pollen samples was taken; unfortunately, the weather conditions hindered an exhaustive investigation. It can, however, be said that the conditions at the site are favourable for a palaeoecological investigation which would probably result in a pollen-analytical dating of the bog body. The work that remains to be done is estimated at 2 men for 14 days or at a rough estimate 1400kr, including travel and labourer assistance.

The Bog Laboratory has written to, respectively, stationmaster Holger Hansen, Bording, and chief librarian Peder Nielsen, Silkeborg, with the result that the peat spade from Silkeborg Museum has been sent here to the museum.

Seven-year-old Ove, son of one of the finders, Emil Højgaard, by the peat baulk where Tollund Man was found. Photographed in 1952 by National Museum staff who carried out a preliminary investigation of the bog stratigraphy. *(Photo: J. Troels-Smith)*

We consider the continued investigation of the find site for Tollund Man to be very important and we therefore request that 1,400kr be reserved for the continued investigation which according to agreement with Emil Højgaard should take place in mid-April.

It is requested that, after examination, if possible drawing and photographing, the peat spade be returned to Silkeborg Museum.

The Bog Laboratory, 7th March 1953

Unfortunately for the two scientists, it seems the money was not granted because by 1953 the new radiocarbon dating method had become a reality with a concomitant dating precision far exceeding that which had been seen previously in prehistoric archaeology.

THE RAISED BOG AS CONSERVATOR

The bogs that yielded all these archaeological finds, before draining and cultivation began in earnest, covered as much as a quarter of Denmark's total area. They can roughly be divided into three types: raised bogs (acid), lowland bogs (calcareous) and a transitional form between the two, plus actual meadowlands. Raised bogs are the most fascinating because the very special conditions within them lead to the preservation of bodies such as that of Tollund Man. In the lowland bogs, and those of transitional form, soft tissues have as a rule disappeared, and bodies deposited here can potentially be found as skeletons or adipocere, if they have not degraded completely. Metal artefacts, found in large quantities at war booty sites such as Illerup and Nydam, can be exceptionally well preserved in lowland bogs, whereas this is not the case in acidic raised bogs where metals may have corroded completely.

The dominant plant of the raised bog is bog moss (*sphagnum*), the leaves of which have a very special structure. Most of the leaf cells are 'empty' and as a consequence the leaves have a fantastic ability to absorb water. As a result, a raised bog is almost always wet to walk on, even in dry summers. The water in raised bogs comes from rainwater, not from mineral-rich ground water.

The nutritive salts required by the bog moss are calcium, magnesium, sodium and potassium. These are contained in fine salt particles derived from sea water which are blown up into the atmosphere during storms; their concentration in rainwater increases with proximity to the sea. Before the advent of industrialisation,

Bog moss (*Sphagnum*). *(Photo: Silkeborg Museum)*

The author at Illerup Ådal with a bog skeleton in the foreground.
(Photo: Silkeborg Museum).

bogs obtained their nitrogen in the form of gas arising from forest fires and the decay of organic material.

Measurements have shown that the annual accumulation of peat in raised bogs can be as much as about 15mm, but pressure from overlying layers results in the depth of the peat deposits only increasing by half of this amount, even when peat growth is greatest.

The compaction results in virtually no oxygen reaching the underlying deposits. As a consequence, the peat and the remains of organisms which lie within it cannot be broken down by aerobic bacteria. Compaction also means that most of the bog bodies which have been found are more or less flattened. Tollund Man's slightly curved nose, which originally pointed downwards in the bog, is the result of pressure exerted from above. Other bog bodies also show the effects of more horizontally directed pressure, probably because a raised bog is highest – and thus also heaviest – in the middle. Gravity will therefore result in outwardly directed pressure originating from the centre of the bog.

Raised bog peat represents one of the most acidic types of sediment. The reason for this is that sphagnum plants produce very small quantities of sulphuric acid and humic acid is also formed uppermost in the peat through anaerobic bacterial decay (methane fermentation) of lignin in the peat.

It has therefore been a commonly accepted explanation for the conserving properties of raised bogs that the acid produced by the bog reduced the pH to 3.6–4, thereby conferring anti-bacterial properties on the bog water. The process is exactly the same as when pickling gherkins in vinegar.

The acidic bog water was also responsible for tanning skin as seen, for example, in the case of Grauballe Man, discovered in 1952. People were so convinced of the truth of this explanation that in the conservation of Grauballe Man at the Aarhus Museum, carried out with the assistance of the Danish Tanners' Association, the tanning process begun by nature was continued and completed. This was achieved by 'pit tanning', a process in which tannic acid, based on an extract from fresh oak bark, is one of the main ingredients. Finally, Grauballe Man was given a month-long stay in a bath of Turkey Red Oil (sulphonated castor oil) followed by a couple of applications of leather dressing, after which he was ready to be exhibited.

When fully tanned in this way, he should – like any piece of ordinary leather – be able to remain stable, given a regular treatment with leather dressing; the use of wax, and problems caused by its subsequent shrinkage after cooling, was thereby avoided.

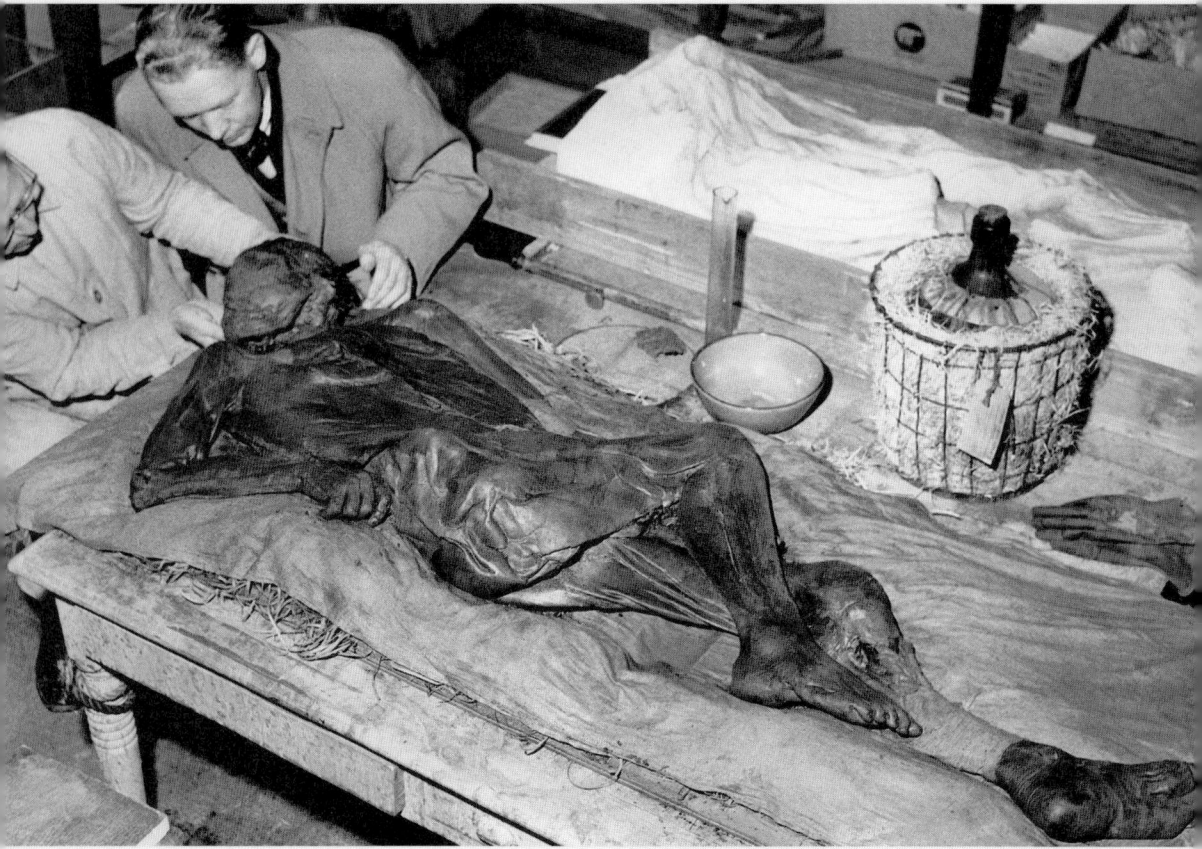

Grauballe Man was tanned under expert guidance as part of the conservation process. *(Photo: P.V. Glob)*

In the longer term, the conservation of Grauballe Man proved to be rather problematic. The process had not, after all, rendered him stable and cracks began to appear, especially in his face.

The innermost secrets behind the conserving properties of the bog have yet to be fully unravelled.

The assumption that it was the acidic bog water which had both a tanning and an anti-bacterial effect was examined in more detail when a bog body was found in Lindow Moss, near Manchester in 1983. Many scientific disciplines became involved in the subsequent research when it was realised that the find represented a unique opportunity to examine the secrets of bog bodies using techniques and analytical methods which were not available in the immediate post-war years when most bodies were discovered.

Even as the first investigations of Lindow Man got underway, the question was raised as to the possibility of conservation so the body could be exhibited at the British Museum. Advice was sought from Danish museums, but it was decided that the methods they had employed should not be applied to Lindow Man.

To summarise, the conservation processes operating in a bog can be described as complex; the presence of several factors is necessary simultaneously for a body to be preserved.

In order for a bog body to be as well preserved as Tollund Man it must first have been carried out into a raised bog and placed in an excavated pit – in most case an already open peat cutting, judging from the finds of contemporary peat spades. This event must take place in winter or in early spring while the bog water is cold, less than 4°C. If the temperature is higher, the internal organs will begin to decay, leading to putrefaction and the formation of gasses. These, in turn, will cause the body to float to the surface of the water, where it will come into contact with oxygen in the air which will quickly initiate a further process of decay. The activities of birds and animals will also contribute to the continuing degradation.

Low temperatures delay the onset of the decay processes to such an extent that the acidic bog water then has the necessary time to penetrate the corpse. Consequently, securing the corpse to the bottom of the pit also promotes the conservation process. This is achieved by a layer of peat being placed, or collapsing, over the body. In some instances hooked sticks were employed to hold the body down. Securing the body could, in practical terms, only take place while the pit was fairly empty of water. The conserving bog water would then quickly flood in from the surrounding peat and cover the corpse and peat growth could resume.

It is clear that some form of securing the body to the bottom of the pit is a characteristic feature of well-preserved bog bodies. If all that was required for successful conservation of a corpse was for someone or something to fall into a water-filled pit in a raised bog on a cold winter's day and drown, then these bogs would be littered with the well-preserved corpses of accidentally drowned deer, foxes, hares etc..

It seems very likely that corpses were also deposited in bogs where nature's conservational abilities were not in evidence, or in raised bogs at times of the year when warm weather led to the conservation process being 'overtaken' by bacterial decay. We cannot be certain of this because, by the very nature of things, the evidence is lacking. However, it could be true in very many instances and it seems likely, given the very complex nature of the process involved, that the bodies which have been preserved and subsequently discovered represent a very small fraction of the total number of bodies treated in this way.

4

DATING

'Gentlemen, radiocarbon dating is not a matter of belief, it is a matter of fact.'

Niels Bohr

While the conservation work was carried out at the National Museum, the people behind Silkeborg Museum were in the process of fitting out part of Silkeborg Hovedgaard, a manor house dating from 1767, as a museum. They shared the building with a kindergarten, Dronning Louises Asyl. The museum's collections had, until then, led a rather chequered existence: at first they were exhibited in an attic above the town's library, then in a building which had previously housed the Veterinary Inspection Office for the meat trade; at times they were simply were packed away.

The original idea was to establish a history and natural history museum combined with an art gallery. Nature was the first to become detached when, in 1963 the collection of stuffed birds was loaned to Th. Langs Skoler, an organisation comprising a school, teacher training college and high school. Art accompanied the museum to Silkeborg Hovedgaard and while the conservation of Tollund Man was underway, the celebrated Danish artist Asger Jorn had the opportunity to exhibit at the new museum. His work, focussing in particular on ceramics inspired by the local pottery tradition, was not universally well received; but this is unlikely to have surprised Jorn. The art gallery first became independent in 1969.

On several occasions during the conservation of Tollund Man, Silkeborg Museum enquired as to how the work was progressing, and almost every time the answer was – it just takes time. A bill for 435kr for conservation of the head and some bronze artefacts from another archaeological site was, however, paid by the museum.

Finally, in June 1952, Silkeborg Museum was able to send a written invitation to Therkel Mathiassen, head of the National Museum's Prehistoric Department, to dinner at Hotel Dania – at the expense of the Museum Society. This was the

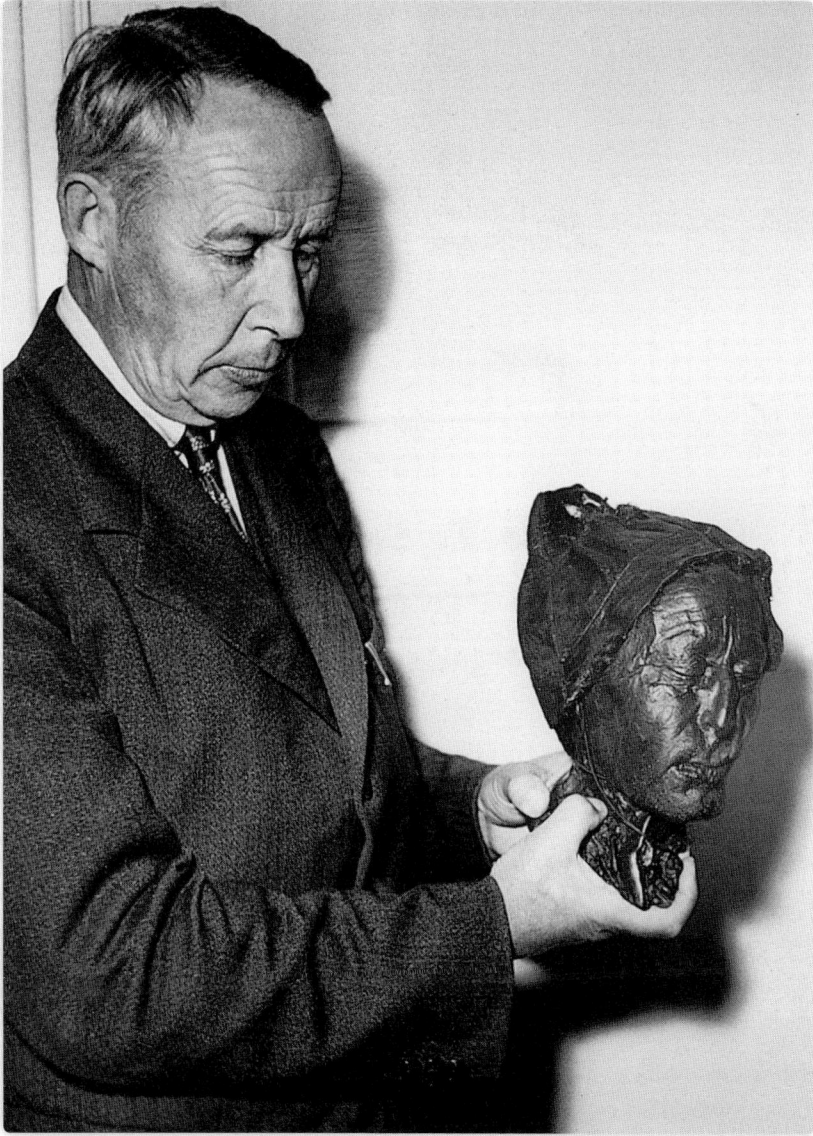

Therkel Mathiassen of the National Museum delivers Tollund Man's head to Silkeborg Museum in 1952. It was almost two years to the day after body was discovered. *(Photo: Niels T. Søndergaard)*

day Mathiassen was to hand over Tollund Man's head. He was, of course, photographed holding the head and the newspapers reported that its appearance was not as macabre as many had probably imagined. Not a word was mentioned about the rest of the body – the press acted as if it had simply disappeared, and they were not alone!

The head was placed in a case designed by the town's leading architect, Knud Sørensen. Made of teak and stainless steel it was both beautiful and simple, following the style of the time. The gallery was, on the other hand, not particularly

P.V. Glob in 1977, standing by the post in Bjældskovdal which marks the find site for Tollund Man. (Photo: Silkeborg Museum)

Grauballe Man immediately after discovery. *(Photo: P. V. Glob)*

attractive and clearly the interior design of the museum was not an important municipal priority: white walls, three fluorescent tubes, draughty windows and situated next to a small toilet. Present-day conservators would have been appalled – pointing out that the light was too intense, the climate too unstable and the case vibrated. However, thanks to the robust conservation process, a detailed check carried out in 1970 was able to reveal that the head had 'survived' its first two decades unaltered.

P.V. Glob's book *The Bog People*, published in 1969, sparked great interest in the find – not least from English-speaking parts of the world: Glob ostensibly addressed his book to fourteen English schoolgirls – and to his own daughter Elsebeth of the same age – but wrote in a way that appealed both to the scholar and the layman.

On several occasions coaches arrived carrying American tourists on so-called 'Fairy Tales Tours' whereby, in addition to visiting Hans Christian Andersen's House, Rosenborg Palace with the crown jewels and the Little Mermaid, they also viewed the little display case in Silkeborg containing Tollund Man's head.

In order to place Tollund Man in his correct cultural-historical setting in the gallery, use was made of Silkeborg Museum's collection of local Iron Age finds. The exhibits dated from the beginning of the Early Iron Age, around 500 BC, to the beginning of the Late Iron Age, around AD 400. Glob's evaluation of Tollund Man as being about 2,000 years old – revealed to the press only days after the discovery – became the focal point around which the exhibition was centred chronologically. There was no more precise date.

In 1975 it was decided to move the kindergarten away from Silkeborg Hovedgaard and the entire building was then at the disposal of the museum.

With the considerable and increasing interest he aroused, it was natural for Tollund Man to be given a central position in the exhibition. He had until that time had a function on a par with an *objet d'art* – beautiful, sleeping – one could stand face to face with the past; but which past exactly was that?

As a step in the revision of the exhibition a new piece of research work was launched. The museum would attempt to fit Tollund Man into the surroundings in which he had lived – villages, houses, fields, cemeteries and, not least, also discover what he could tell us, indirectly, about his time; in particular why he had been hung and deposited at the bottom of a peat bog by his contemporaries.

The author, by then appointed as the museum's first professionally trained archaeologist, had not received much assistance in his studies aimed at explaining the phenomenon of Tollund Man to museum visitors. One would think that archaeologists would recognise bog bodies as an easy shortcut to an understanding of the everyday lives of prehistoric people, how they had styled their hair, what they ate, etc. – but it was almost as if it was too easy and, consequently, bordering on the unscientific.

The fact that bog bodies could reveal aspects of past religions involving human sacrifices clearly lay off-limits and religion was borderline taboo in university archaeology departments. P.V. Glob was one of the first archaeologists to address the subject of bog bodies seriously and to attempt to arrive at a religious interpretation of their fate. But this did not bring much recognition in Copenhagen, either at the National Museum or the University; revered institutions located beneath the same roof.

A corresponding lack of innovative thinking was also shown by several archaeologists when a new method of dating was introduced which, in the long term, would revolutionise archaeology: radiocarbon dating. This method came into use in Denmark in 1953 and a recently-discovered bog body, Grauballe Man, found in 1952 very close to Silkeborg, was the first of many which would subsequently be dated in this much more precise way. In this case, the method was able to demonstrate that Grauballe Man was not, in fact, Røde Kristian – a man who, a couple of generations earlier, had left a nearby inn, Svostrup Kro, in high spirits and was never seen again. Even though several of the locals had 'identified' him, Glob was able to make the triumphant announcement that Røde Kristian had been defeated by the atoms. When the head of the Radiocarbon Dating Laboratory, civil engineer Henrik Tauber, telephoned and told him the result: an Iron Age man, Glob replied: 'I damn well knew it!'

The foundation for radiocarbon dating was developed by Professor W.F. Libby in 1947–51; a piece of work which brought him the Nobel Prize in 1960. An interest in atomic physics, originally predominantly of military application, could also be used here for a civil purpose.

The Radiocarbon Dating Laboratory in Copenhagen was the first to be established outside the USA. It was directly associated with the National Museum, but was also available to other research fields, including geology. Archaeologists are conservative by nature and the idea of a dating laboratory had to be allowed to mature for quite a while, before it was properly accepted. In early 1951, a meeting was arranged between physicists, archaeologists and geologists to discuss the possibility of establishing a radiocarbon laboratory in Denmark. Civil engineer Henrik Tauber, who subsequently became head of the laboratory, recalls that the discussion quickly became focussed on whether one really dared believe the results of this new and, in many ways, fantastic dating method. That was until a gentleman in the front row turned to half-face those behind and in his characteristic low voice said: 'Gentlemen, radiocarbon dating is not a matter of belief; it is a matter of fact!' His name was Niels Bohr – and with that the question was settled.

On a blackboard, the principles behind the radiocarbon dating method are relatively simple. Carbon is one of the earth's building blocks and is found in all living organisms. The radioactive isotope of carbon, ^{14}C, is formed from nitrogen, which makes up 80 per cent of the earth's atmosphere. When cosmic radiation enters the earth's atmosphere, a change occurs in the energy of the atmosphere and one of the results of this is that neutrons are created. These subsequently

Grauballe Man immediately after discovery. The facial skin is heavily folded; a consequence of his throat having been cut. Even so, he was 'identified' by local people as the missing Røde Kristian. (Photo: P.V. Glob)

enter into a reaction with nitrogen and, as a consequence, one of the products is radioactive carbon – 14C. Via the atmosphere and through absorption in sea water 14C is distributed evenly around the globe. It is taken up by plants via photosynthesis and these in turn are eaten by animals and humans which consequently also then contain 14C. As a result, at any given point in time, the quantity of radioactive carbon is the same in all living organisms anywhere around the globe. When an organism dies it no longer takes up carbon, and as 14C is radioactive the amount present in its tissues declines due to radioactive decay. Accordingly, the smaller the residue of 14C, the greater the age of the dead material. It has been calculated that only half of the radioactive carbon remains after a period of 5,730 years. The non-radioactive carbon remains unchanged. Radioactive 14C atoms constitute an extremely small proportion of the total amount of carbon; 1 million tons of pure carbon contains only a single gram of radioactive 14C. Therefore, neither we nor Tollund Man and Grauballe Man need worry about dangerous radiation from that source.

The relationship between non-radioactive and radioactive carbon was considered to be constant when the method was first developed. However, Professor Libby knew already in 1951 that, although the basis for the method was sound, a series of complex error sources was inherent in the process.

One of the most serious of these was that the sample material could be contaminated with carbon from the surroundings: This could enter via roots growing down into the sample material from overlying layers – humus compounds derived from decaying plant material could be absorbed and carbonates from the ground water could precipitate out in samples.

The method was also based on there being, in the natural state, a dynamic equilibrium between the different carbon atoms, but this later proved to be not entirely true. The proportion of 14C relative to non-radioactive carbon could vary by as much as 1.5 per cent. However, if the magnitude of these fluctuations was known the error could be eliminated. Fortunately, the deviations could be measured year by year in the annual rings of trees because, as the name suggests, a new tree ring is formed each year containing the carbon proportions for that year. Among the trees used in 1954 for these corrections was a collection of pine trees, Pinus aristata, or bristle cone pine, which grows on the border between California and Nevada. Even though these trees were not particularly large or impressive it quickly became apparent that some of them were very ancient, up to almost 5,000 years old, and they were still alive with green shoots. There were also some even older dead trees in the area. These enabled the tree-ring sequences from the living trees to be extended even further back in time by exploiting the overlap between the two.

The variation in 14C could now be established and taken into account and the dates corrected accordingly. This work is still ongoing today, resulting in progressively more and more exact dates.

A more tangible error with respect to the early dates arose from problems caused by contaminant material penetrating samples, and the limited possibilities for removing this contamination – but the situation would subsequently improve.

The first radiocarbon dates for Tollund Man were produced as late as 1977 and the results were not without drama. In a preliminary telephone call to the author, the head of the Radiocarbon Dating Laboratory, Henrik Tauber, revealed that Tollund Man was not 2,000 years old, as Glob had stated, but only half that age – he was a Viking!

While we waited for days for a further date (a 'b sample'), there was ample opportunity to speculate on how the news should be broken to a probably very astonished public.

Before it came to that, however, the author again received a telephone call from the Radiocarbon Dating Laboratory: there was something wrong with the equipment – contamination with radioactive radon had taken place – yet another source of error. The replacement of a spare part had led to this increased radiation level. When the contaminating radioactive source was removed, the sample of Tollund Man must, correspondingly, become older. The correct date came – almost to the day – on the 25th anniversary of Tollund Man's exhibition at Silkeborg Museum, and it revealed that he was from around 220 BC and thereby perhaps as much as 700 years older than Grauballe Man.

Many people are surprised that the date for Tollund Man's death has changed in recent years, but this is due to improvements in the dating method which permit correction of the age provided by the original radiocarbon date. Instead of recalculating all radiocarbon dates each time new and more precise measurements of the tree-ring series provide small corrections, so-called calibration curves are produced. These enable the old dates (which are now referred to as conventional radiocarbon dates) to be directly converted to new revised dates based on the latest information. The resulting dates are called calibrated radiocarbon dates and, over the course of time, this refinement process has altered Tollund Man's original radiocarbon date by about 200 years. We are now confident that his time of death lies between 375 and 210 BC, but further minor changes must still be expected.

As the other radiocarbon dates for bog bodies produced over time were almost all roughly the same as that for Tollund Man, Grauballe Man suddenly stood out as being exceptionally late. His was the first bog body to which the method was applied. Any talk of a lost drunk, Røde Kristian, was excluded as the Geiger counter revealed that of the original 14C which Grauballe Man had absorbed when alive, 81.5 per cent still remained. This corresponded to his death being in the period between 1530 and 1740 years before 1950, i.e. between AD 210 and 410; he lived in the Late Roman Iron Age.

The question was whether the dated sample could have become contaminated in some way in the bog by later carbon-rich material percolating downwards. An enquiry from Silkeborg Museum brought the response that this source of error had not been taken into consideration. The time was therefore ripe for a new date in recognition of the fact that bog bodies represent some of the most difficult material to date because humus compounds etc. originating from the bog easily become bound up in skin and tissue. As the peat which accumulates over the

The AMS dating laboratory is housed in a cellar beneath the University of Aarhus. *(Photo: Ingelise Vinther Andersen)*

body will, by the very nature of things, be younger, any material which moves downwards from here will cause the date for the body to be artificially late.

The new sample received the most extensive treatment the laboratory had, up until that point, applied to a sample from a bog body. In the course of this, 80 per cent of the material was dissolved and extracted. The date was, accordingly, produced on the remaining 20 per cent of the sample. After this very drastic treatment, the laboratory staff were confident that the result must be very close to the correct date.

As expected, the date following the new pre-treatment was almost 400 years older than the original date and the time of Grauballe Man's death now became fixed at *c.* 55 BC.

In parallel with everyday work at the Radiocarbon Dating Laboratory, a completely new technique was developed for determining the total number of 14C atoms present in a sample. This was achieved with the aid of large particle accelerators and the application of mass spectrometry (the AMS technique). The size of the analytical equipment required is comparable with an inter-city train.

Using the AMS technique it is now possible to date very small samples, as little as 1/1000 of that previously required. Instead of a normal sample comprising 5–10g of wood or charcoal, a few milligrams now suffice. This opens up completely new opportunities because, where previously it was often necessary to sacrifice an entire femur, a few hairs are now enough.

Grauballe Man had once again to provide sample material, this time for an AMS date. The result, together with new calibrations, added almost a further 300 years to his age. He now dates from 350 BC and, in terms of age, has come into line with most of the other bog bodies. However, he has become far removed chronologically from the Roman literary sources which Glob, among others, had used to describe the fate he and the other bog bodies suffered.

5

FURTHER BODIES FROM THE BOG

With the development of a new radiocarbon dating technique, for which even small samples of the order of a couple of hairs were sufficient for a secure date and at a cost which was affordable, the path was clear for more detailed investigations of bog bodies. Researchers had previously virtually stumbled forward in the dark – was the term 'bog body' appropriate to all finds of human remains in bogs, ranging from skulls to entire well-preserved human corpses with skin and hair and wearing clothes? Was the term 'bog body' also appropriate for finds of people from all countries? Should anyone who ended up in a bog – from the Mesolithic Koelbjerg Woman on Funen to the Second World War airmen who crashed in the Masurian Lakes west of Gdansk – be considered a bog body? That would, of course, be absurd. Following the production of a large number of dates for bodies found in bogs, those from the Late Neolithic and from the Early Iron Age appear clearly to be in the majority.

Some of these people probably drowned one cold winter day, or their corpse was thrown into a lake and had drifted around in the ice until it was stranded on the lake shore. Others, or parts of them, were found together with pottery vessels, parts of wagons and ox skulls, which had been placed as offerings on the contemporary bog surface. These situations clearly differ so markedly from that of Tollund Man that a common explanation seems unlikely.

Other bog bodies are so similar in their circumstances to Tollund Man that there must be a link. This conclusion is supported by the fact that the radiocarbon dates reveal a group of people in the Celtic Iron Age who, like Tollund Man, were killed and deposited in a peat cutting, often wearing a skin cape or with one placed beside them.

There are, of course, some bodies which are either a century or so earlier or later, and occasional examples which are much older or much younger. However, most of the bodies which Glob proclaimed to be members of the 'bog people' fall into same category.

In connection with the renovation of Silkeborg Museum in 1977 and, as a consequence, a new location for Tollund Man's head, the intention was to place him in context, surrounded by archaeological finds from the period to which he had now been dated. The circumstances of his discovery were also to be described in more detail. So the museum returned once more to Bjældskovdal, where the finders, neighbours and former peat cutters were still able to provide new and previously unrevealed details about the discovery which had now taken place more than twenty-five years previously. In parallel with this investigation it was also the museum's aim to be able to provide further information for the, by this time, very numerous foreign colleagues, writers and poets who had been inspired by Glob's book. The questions most often asked, frequently in a slightly critical tone, were: 'Where is the rest of Tollund Man?' – 'Wasn't there also another bog body, the one Glob describes as a man with a hair-do?'

The answer I had been forced to give in response was: 'I am afraid they have gone missing!' With respect to the latter bog body – which the discoverers of Tollund Man had already vaguely heard about – his/her skin cape is still in the National Museum's collection, but in a poor state of preservation. Even so, Silkeborg Museum could fruitfully begin some new research.

In her doctoral thesis from 1950 'Olddanske Tekstiler' ('Ancient Danish Textiles') Margrethe Hald only describes the find cursorily as the focus of her work was textiles, not leather. She is not exactly impressed by the garment which she characterises as follows:

> The skin which was found proved to be from a cape similar to the previously mentioned pieces found in bogs; it is however too fragmented for a drawing to be of any interest, and it does not reveal anything new. The sewing is executed in running stitch and with thread of leather. The cape itself is of sheep skin, perhaps with sewn-on pieces of cow hide.

The corpse was mentioned briefly in Glob's *The Bog People* and in Thorkil Ramskou's book 'Noget om Hår og Skæg' ('On Hair and Beards'). These two authors were both interested primarily in the corpse's braided hairstyle. They are of the view that the corpse is that of a man, based on the fact that men have been found in Northern

Germany with their hair in 'Swabian knots', corresponding to Roman descriptions of the hairstyle worn by men of the German tribe the Swabians, who lived in Northern Europe. In her book *Frisurer fra ældre jernalder, mosefund og gravfund* ('Early Iron Age Hairstyles, from Bog Bodies and Burials'), Elisabeth Munksgaard sees the body as being female, an evaluation also based on the hairstyle.

So there was enough to begin with: The corpse lay near Tollund Man – was this coincidence? Were they from the same period? Was it the body of a man or a woman and how did they die? Was it the same fate that had befallen Tollund Man? Could the hairstyle and the clothing provide new information?

Fortune favoured the new research work. The discoverers of the body, Jens and Jenny Zakariassen, were still alive, and the bog body itself proved still to exist, in a desiccated state, in the National Museum's stores. Jysk Medicinhistorisk Selskab (The Society of Medical History of Jutland) had just been formed and was more than willing to take care of the more detailed medical examinations, and there was also the possibility of obtaining a precise date.

The two finders, husband and wife, recalled that during peat cutting in 1938 they encountered what they took, in the first instance, to be the body of a drowned animal. Even so, they contacted farmer Søren Jensen who was renowned for his interest in archaeology. Søren Jensen, better known as Søren Wollesen, as well as being a farmer was also the manager of the local telephone exchange, so everybody knew him, and he knew everybody.

After Søren Jensen had dug further in Bjældskovdal, he contacted the National Museum, and on 23 June 1938 museum curator H.C. Broholm arrived at the site. Broholm carried out a detailed investigation of the discovery and a set of excavation plans and a reasonably detailed report resulted from his excavation:

> From farmer Søren Jensen, Funder, on 20th June 1938 the National Museum received a message that a corpse had been found wrapped in animal hide in a bog belonging to farmer Jens Zachariassen, Elling. On 23rd June the find site was investigated.
>
> The corpse, which was found during peat cutting, lay in an approximate N-S direction with the feet towards the south and it was enclosed in a skin with short hair. When it was unearthed, Søren Jensen was summoned and he had the unfortunate idea that it was a roe deer, and dug the legs and lower body almost completely away, and only when he encountered a shred of woven cloth did he stop digging and inform the museum.
>
> The corpse was, accordingly, very damaged when the investigation took place; but it was clear that it had been buried in a pit in the bog because the wall of the pit was very clear to the west.

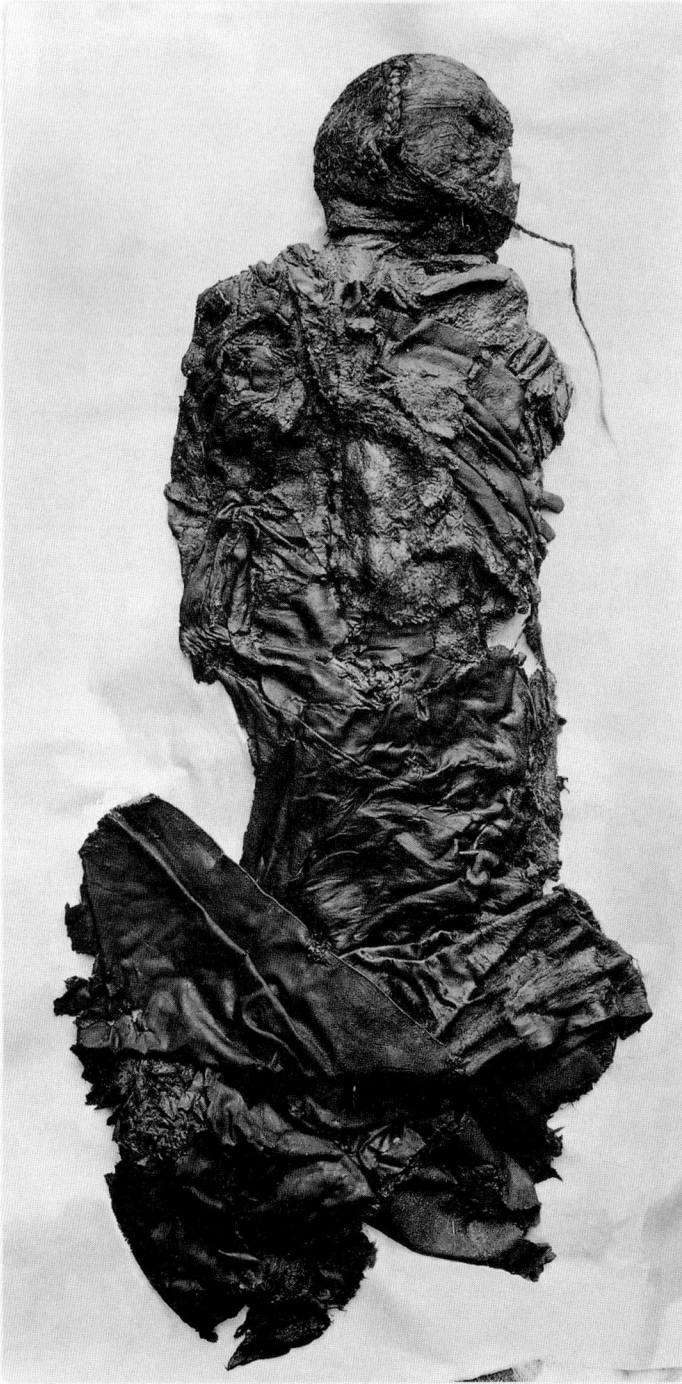

Elling Woman's badly damaged back exposed at the National
Museum. *(Photo: The National Museum)*

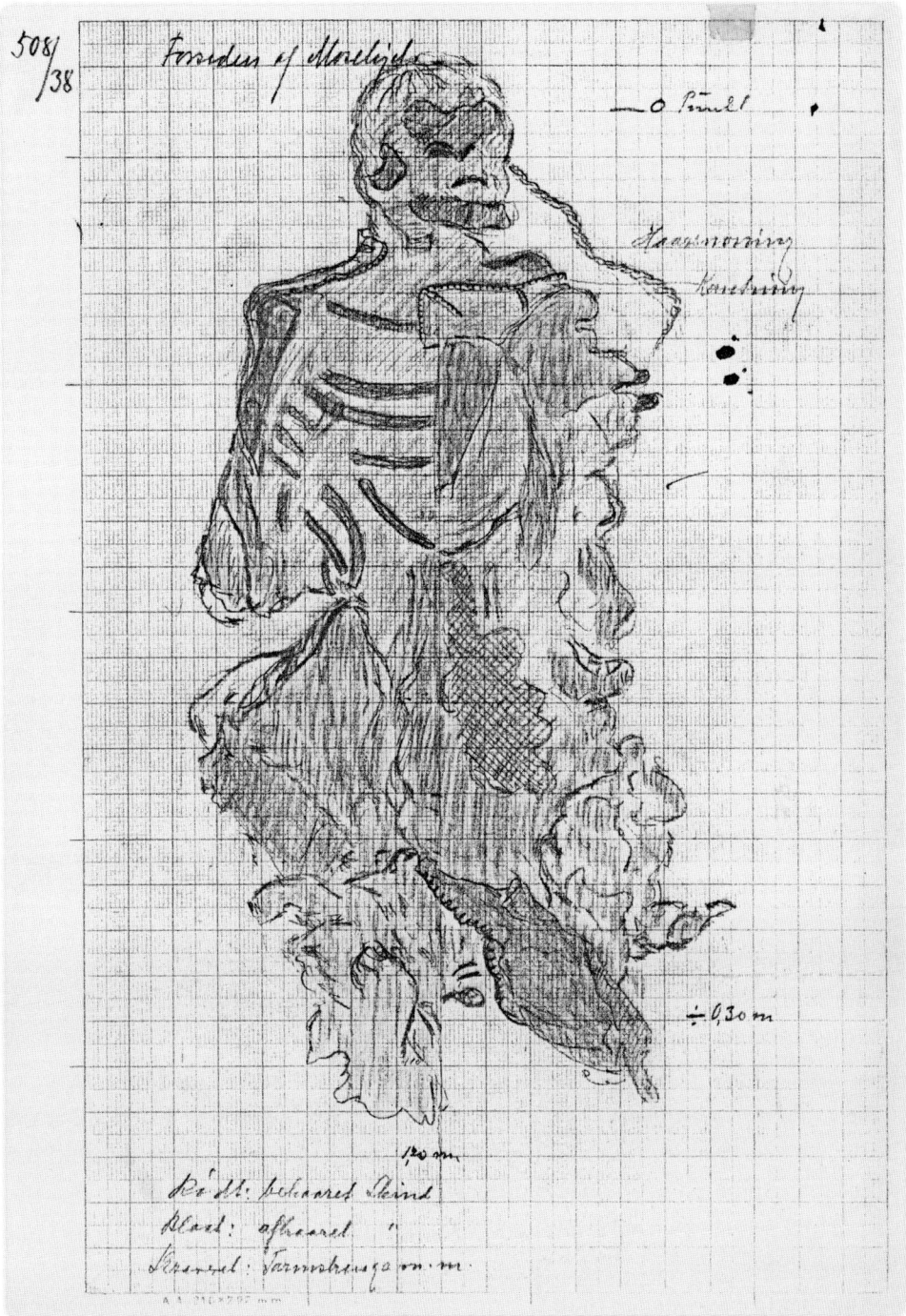

Elling Woman from the front with an attempt at identifying the parts of her clothing. *(Drawing: Miss Frederiksen, the National Museum)*

The head of the deceased lay c. 36cm above the sandy base of the bog within a distinct peat layer, 60cm further south lay the skin only 15cm above the base of the bog. Over the place where the corpse lay the surface of bog had long ago been cut away, but it was preserved 3–4m further south, and with the aid of a tape measure and spirit level the depth of the skull beneath the original bog surface was determined as being 155cm, and the base of the bog lay accordingly c. 190cm beneath the surface.

The corpse was enclosed within a plaster cast and was uncovered in the laboratory by conservator J. Raklev and Miss Frederiksen, who executed drawings of its position and of the clothing. Peat samples for pollen analysis were taken by Dr J. Iversen.

Copenhagen 4th December 1938
H.C. Broholm

Apart from that outlined by the report, no further examinations were carried out on the body. The leather clothing was conserved together with the woven belt which had prompted the involvement of archaeologists. Photographs were unfortunately not taken of the body in the bog, only of Søren Jensen who, together with a box containing parts of the body, is seen displaying a leather cord with a loop which was found with the corpse.

In 1978, Jens Zakariassen recalled that it took three days to recover the body from the bog. The museum curator from the National Museum arrived the day after the find was reported in order to take charge of the work. A careful excavation was carried out around the body so that it then lay within a block of peat, so to speak. The local carpenter, Ejnar Lunding, who twelve years later also supplied the timber for the crate in which Tollund Man was packed, made a wooden board which was pushed under the peat block. Everything was then encapsulated within a plaster cast inside a wooden crate, which was transported to Funder station. Jens Zakariassen, his wife Jenny, a man by the name of Rudolf and others lent a hand.

He could also recall that close to the bog body, within a radius of about 25m, a T-shaped peat spade was found in addition to another wooden implement; these were later submitted to Them Museum. Jens Zakariassen was in no doubt that the corpse had been buried so that it almost sat upright in the grave. The hole had not been very big.

After being excavated at the National Museum, the body was apparently put to one side and allowed to dry out.

Despite forty years of oblivion in a museum store it was, remarkably, still possible to carry out a thorough investigation of the body and its clothing. To this end a

Farmer, telephone exchange manager and amateur archaeologist Søren Jensen with 'detached body parts' resulting from his first 'excavation' of Elling Woman. *(Photo: Funder Local History Archive)*

team was assembled which, in addition to the author from Silkeborg Museum, comprised forensic pathologist Markil Gregersen, radiologists Bendt Langfeldt and Jørn Raahede and, for an investigation of the teeth, forensic odontologist H.P. Philipsen, all from Aarhus. Collaboration between archaeologists and medical science had been seen before but never on such a comprehensive scale.

This signalled the start of extensive new investigations of a large number of the bog bodies kept in store rooms or displayed in exhibitions at Danish Museums; one body even resided in a church. Corpses which had been investigated previously, including Grauballe Man and Tollund Man, were also subjected to new

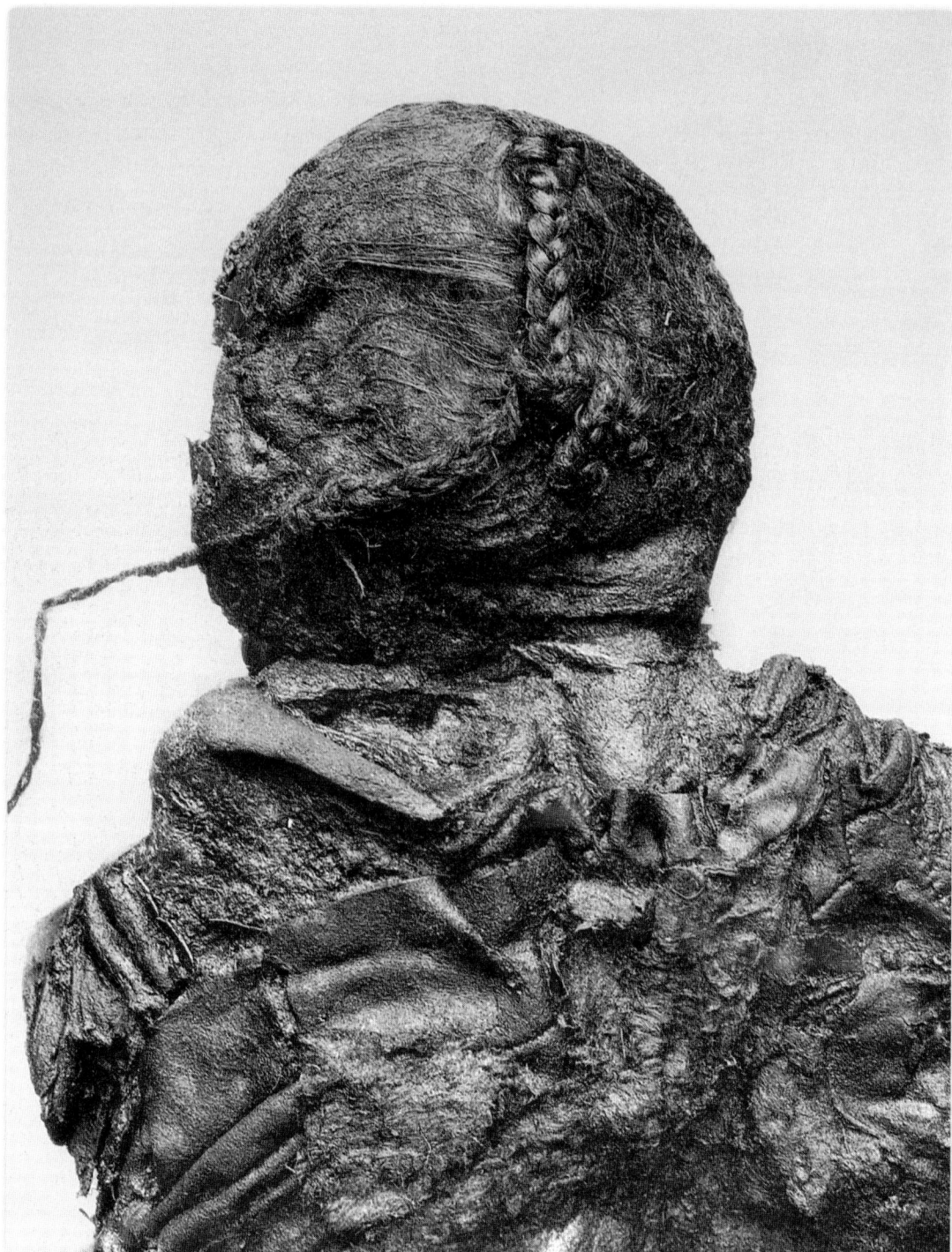

The hanging furrow around the neck of Elling Woman can be clearly seen on photographs taken during the investigations in 1938. *(Photo: The National Museum)*

examinations, whereby the most recent medical advances, both in knowledge and technology, could be applied.

The new examination of the body recovered from Bjældskovdal in 1938 began with radiocarbon dating which revealed that the corpse had been deposited in the bog between 360 and 200 BC, i.e. in the Early Iron Age. This date opened up the possibility that the corpse was a contemporary of Tollund Man – they could even have known each other. That much was clear.

The cause of death could readily be established by the doctors as a 'hanging furrow' was clearly visible around the neck on the photographs taken at the

Søren Jensen holding the leather halter which very probably was used in the hanging of Elling Woman. *(Photo: Funder Local History Archive)*

National Museum in 1938. As the accompanying finds also included a leather halter, of a width corresponding to that of the furrow, there was not much doubt about the cause of death. The leather halter was that with which Søren Jensen was photographed, together with other parts of the bog body. It must have been torn from the body when he, or Jens Zakariassen, struck it with a spade. Loose human hairs adhering to the halter show that the latter must have been close to the corpse's hair or hairline. The hanging furrow is so clear on the photograph that the halter must have sat very tightly about the neck of the corpse until it was hit by a modern spade.

The bones of the corpse showed that the right side had been exposed to pressure from the overlying peat. The deceased was a woman of about twenty-five to thirty years of age and on the part of the body which remained undamaged following its less than gentle recovery no further injuries or signs of illness could be identified. In the first instance the body was given the name Elling Girl, but in view of her age, the name Elling Woman is probably more correct.

The colour of her hair today is dark red. Its original colour has not been established, but it is evident from other bog bodies that the bog has a colouring effect on the hair, normally resulting in a red colour. Elling Woman's hair is, however, significantly darker than that observed on other bog bodies and this could indicate that she was a brunette.

The hairstyle, which up until this point had been misinterpreted, emerged unscathed from these vicissitudes. The misinterpretation probably arose from the fact that an interpretation was based exclusively on the photographs taken when the corpse was discovered and these give the impression of there being several plaits. Closer examination of the hair revealed that there was, in reality, only one plait and that the coiffure was on the whole very simple, although sufficiently difficult that the woman presumably needed assistance in doing her hair. This was true at least of the living model employed in an experimental reconstruction. At the same time it also became clear that a considerable head of hair is required – almost a metre in length – a rare sight today even among those with long hair.

The hair is first combed backwards over the top of the head where – about 10cm back from the hairline of the forehead – it is plaited together into a tight, three-stranded plait. This is continued down along the middle of the head to the back of the neck, the combed-together hair of which is progressively included. The character then changes: now the hair is divided into seven twisted pigtails which are combined into three bundles, two containing two strands and one containing three, and the plait is then continued for more than 30cm down the back where ultimately it ends in a knot. One of the bundles of hair strands is used to make the

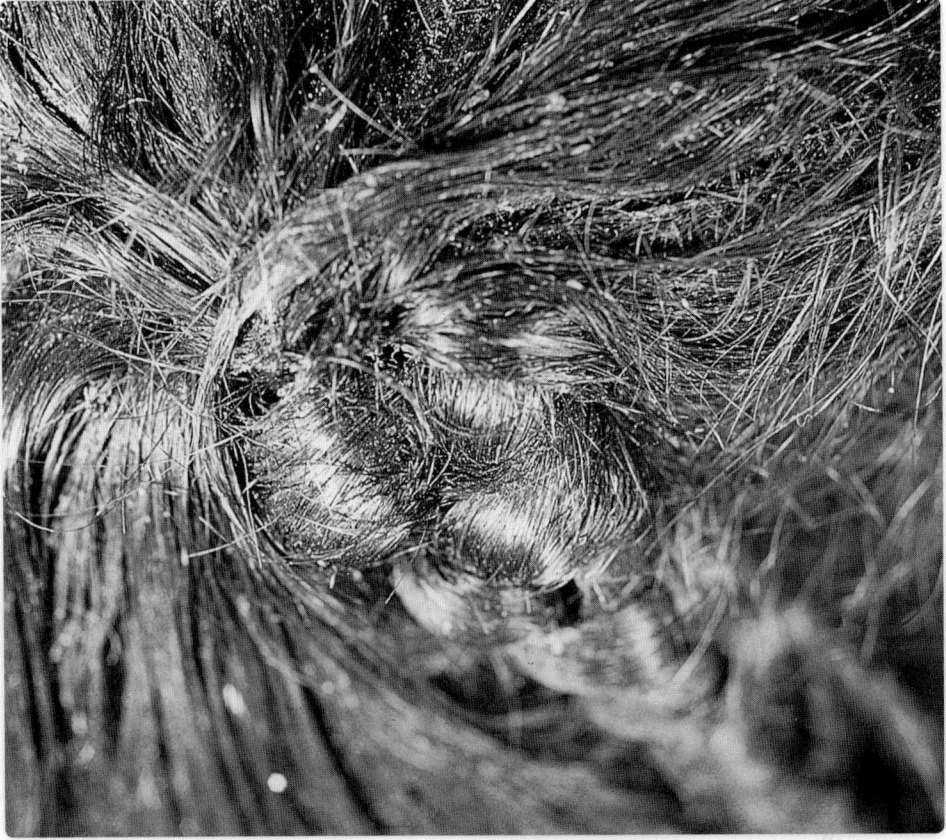

Elling Woman's hair – un-conserved but well preserved. *(Photo: Silkeborg Museum)*

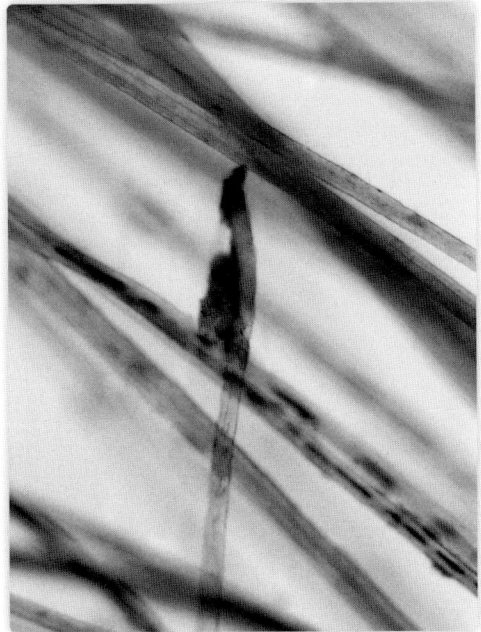

Louse egg in Elling Woman's hair. *(Photo: Silkeborg Museum)*

Reconstruction of Elling Woman's hairstyle. *(Reconstruction and photo: Silkeborg Museum)*

knot, the others continue in a twist which possibly also ended in a knot, unless the ends were allowed to hang loose. The total length of the plait from the top of the head to its end is 80cm. It was used to form a bun at the back of the neck by twisting the loose section twice around the part that runs from the top of the head to the back of the neck. A free-hanging length of about 50cm then remains: a fine hairstyle for a long vigorous head of hair!

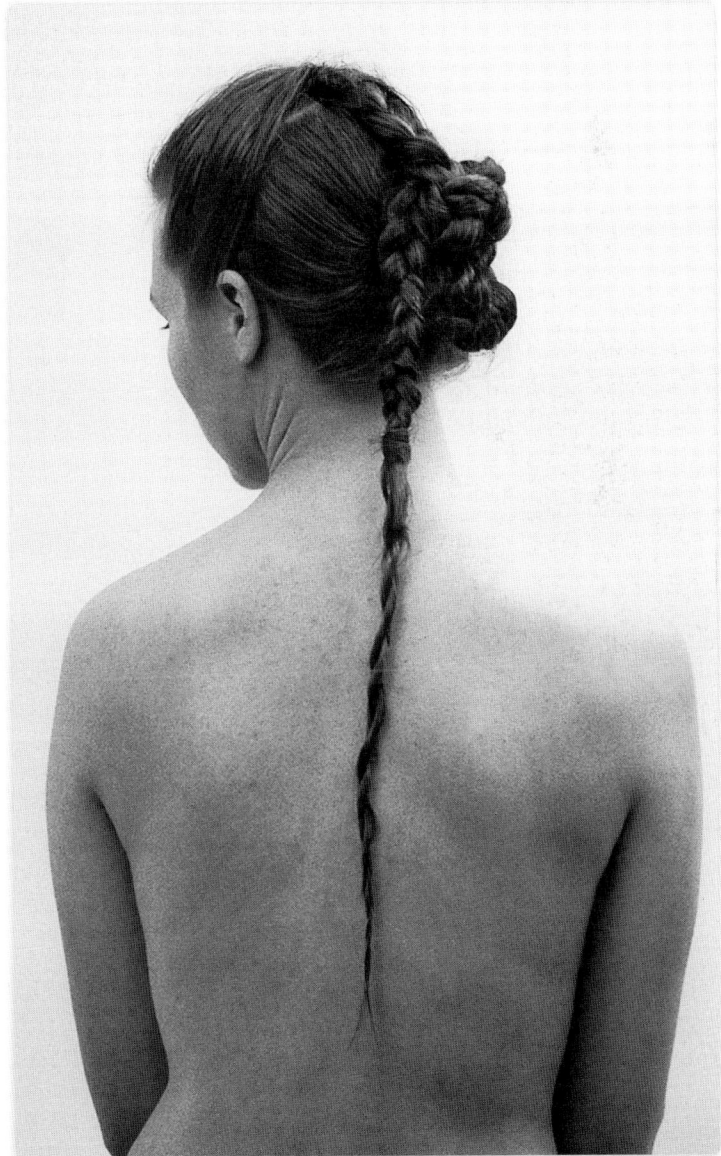

The hairstyle as it was worn by Elling Woman when she was laid in the bog. The model's hair is slightly thicker than that of Elling Woman, but the hair length is the same. *(Photo: Silkeborg Museum)*

The leather attire comprised two parts: a cape which the woman was wearing and another which was wrapped around her legs. The cape she wore was sewn together from several pieces of hide and formed in such a way that from a narrow shoulder section it flared out downwards. The front edge of the cape was reinforced by the hide being laid double. This continued up to the neck opening where there were small holes to take the tie-string, a leather cord, which held the cape together at the front and of which remnants were still preserved. A knee-length cape of this type appears to have been an established part of the Early Iron Age wardrobe, judging from what has been found on and near bog bodies.

The much-damaged cape wrapped around her legs was of ox hide, sewn together using a coarse technique relative to that used on the cape she was wearing. There were some broken straps, the purpose of which cannot immediately be explained, but the item could of course have had many uses before it ended up as a shroud.

Finally, there was the belt of woven wool. This was 4cm wide and 67cm long. The yarn from which the belt was woven is of sheep's wool and is Z-spun. The colour of the belt today is brown, but this is due to colouring effect of the bog water. Based on the above measurements the woman was considered to have been slender, so it was quite a surprise when, in 2006, another piece of the belt turned up which, virtually inexplicably, had been incorporated into Viborg Museum's collections with no accompanying finds data. However, the dimensions, spinning technique and colour are identical. I am willing to hazard a guess that it was Søren Jensen who handed over the piece to the museum in Viborg, because other pieces of the corpse's leather cape have also turned up as gifts to his friends, complete with his greetings.

In the summer of 1978, I met the finders of Tollund Man and Elling Woman out in the bog, because the results of the new medical investigations and the dates had just become available. They were accompanied by another bog character, Tobias Lassen, a haulage contractor and peat merchant who had a detailed knowledge of the bog. He brought remarkable news which would make any archaeologist prick up his ears. There had been yet another discovery of a body in the bog, as well as a bridge or a road running across it, directly past the find sites.

Tobias Lassen recalled that it happened the same year that Charles Lindbergh became the first aviator to fly across the Atlantic (20 May 1927).

On the day Tobias Lassen made his discovery, he had gone down into the bottom of a deep 'pit cut', the base of which lay at a depth of about 5m, in order to extract the last of the peat before the pit was abandoned. Then he discovered a piece of skin. He decided it was probably from a drowned animal and just threw it to one side.

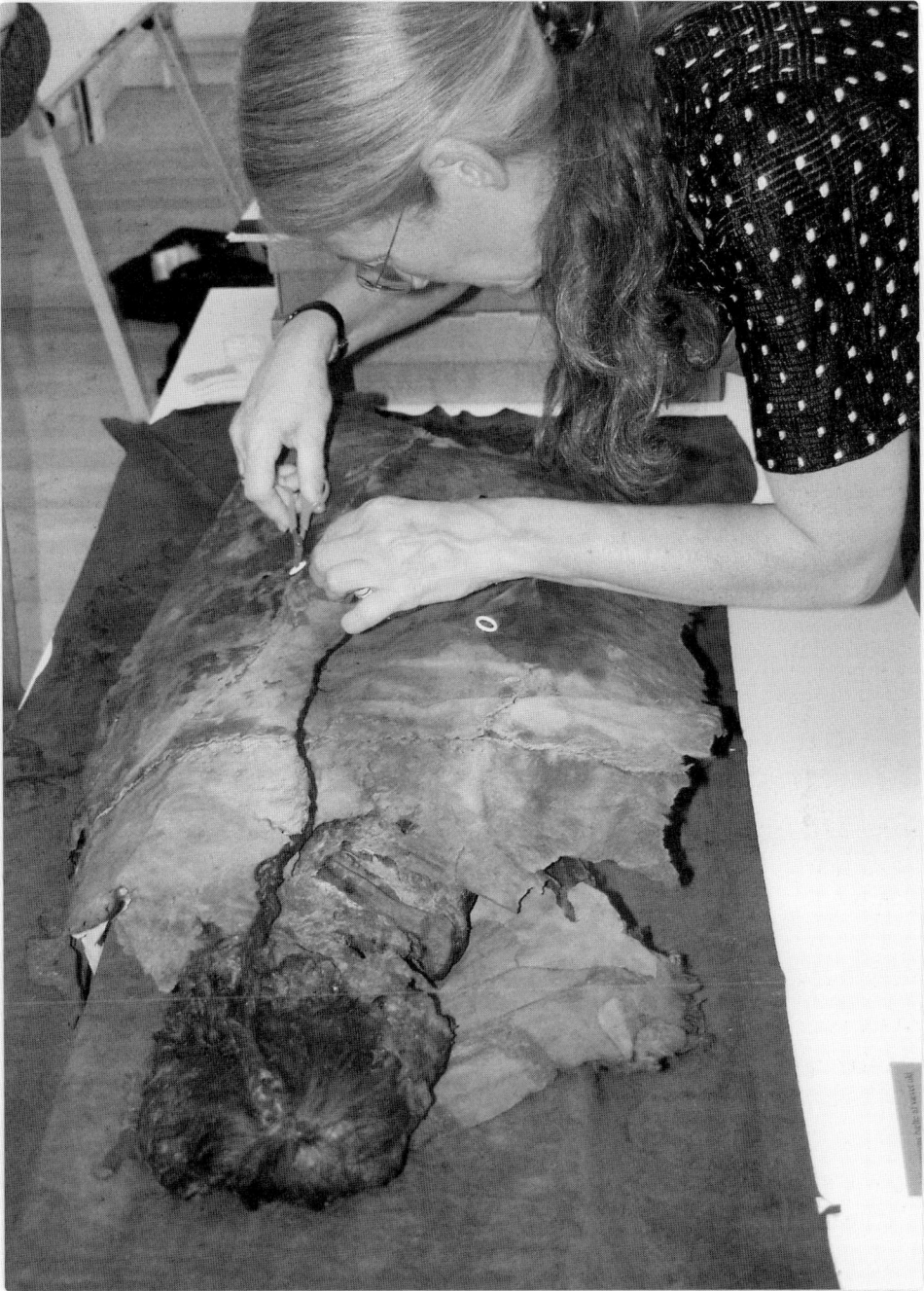

New investigations of Elling Woman's clothing were carried out in 2006 by a group of experts from the Centre for Textile Research, The SAXO Institute, University of Copenhagen. Conservator Anne Lisbeth Schmidt of the National Museum is shown here at work. The group included in the investigations a previously unknown piece of the woven belt. This had inexplicably ended up in the collections of Viborg Museum. *(Photo: Silkeborg Museum)*

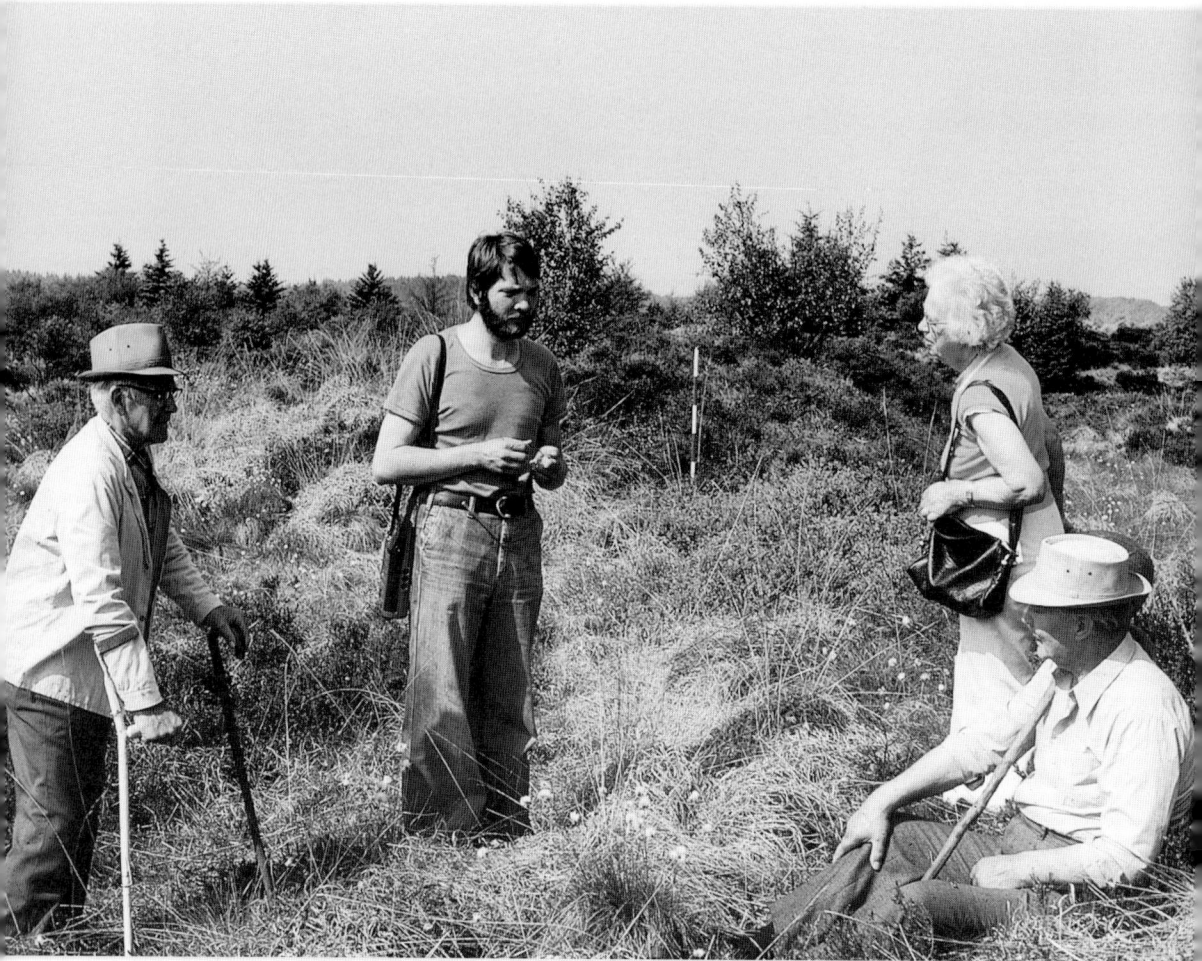

In 1978 the author met the finders of Elling Woman, Jenny and Jens Zakariassen, in Bjældskovdal. Standing on the author's right is Tobias Lassen who owned a peat-extraction business and who found a bog body in 1927 as well as a wooden road across the bog. He still had a post from the road in his woodshed. *(Photo: Silkeborg Museum)*

When Tobias Lassen wanted to continue digging, he was warned by a peat worker who advised him to get out as quickly as possible. The water pressure from the wet peat behind the sides of the pit was dangerously high. Before long the water would cause the sides of the pit to collapse inwards. But Tobias Lassen steadfastly continued his task and found a further piece of skin and later some bones. He was in no doubt that these were human ribs. Suddenly the water began to pour into the cutting and he had to make a swift exit.

The discovery of the pieces of skin and ribs – and the flood – took place in early August, by which time the work of peat cutting should actually have been finished if the peat was to dry before the humidity of autumn.

Next spring, when peat cutting was resumed, the piece of skin was retrieved. It was described as having measured approximately 80 x 60cm, and being almost rectangular in shape. There was still hair on one side, while the other was smooth. There were sewing holes along two of the sides. It was put behind a building where it was subsequently seen by some people from the National Museum who did not, however, take particular note of it, Tobias Lassen recalled.

He knew full well he had made a mistake in not marking the site of his discovery properly so that it could be returned to later. He had once also found a couple of wooden paddles which he took home. When some museum staff later declared these paddles to be of interest due to their shape, one was sent over to the National Museum where, however, it is no longer to be found. His finds were probably a couple of peat spades of 'double paddle' type.

Tobias Lassen also recalled that the peat cutters had found vertical posts standing in the bog, possibly the remains of a bridge or a road. They were preparing the bog for a new season and were removing the uppermost layer in the area where they intended to cut peat. As they did so, vertical sharpened oak posts turned up in two parallel rows. The posts in the rows came every metre or so and the rows were spaced about a couple of metres apart. The upper ends had decayed away, but once down in the actual peat the posts were very well preserved. The hammered-in posts stood at regular intervals which were so precise that the peat cutters could point to where they expected the next post to appear. The bridge could be followed all the way across the bog. Some of the original tree trunks had been so large that they had been cloven longitudinally and it was characteristic of all of them that they were sharpened at their lower end. In a few cases, oblique cuts had been made in the posts.

Lassen pointed to where the bridge or, more probably, the wooden corduroy road, had lain in the bog. It started at the end of a sunken road leading down to the bog and then ran across it towards the western end of the ridge which borders the northern side of the bog. The area has numerous roads which are linked to the Hærvej, the ancient drove road south of Bølling Lake. The route of the bridge/road can be readily fitted into this network. Similar structures are also known in the neighbourhood where vertical wooden posts have secured a log road laid across the springy surface of the bog.

Lassen said the wooden posts were so well preserved that the peat cutters took them home for fuel. A couple of days later he telephoned and said he still had

A modern wooden pathway over the wet bog largely follows the course of the prehistoric road.
(Photo: Silkeborg Museum)

one of the posts in his woodshed which had not been burnt and asked 'whether Silkeborg Museum wanted it?'

Of course Silkeborg Museum wanted it and shortly afterwards an approximately 1m long oak post, which had been sharpened at one end with a metal axe, was brought to the museum. The uppermost part had rotted away. However, the post required no conservation; it had lain untreated for about fifty years in a woodshed, so nothing further could happen to it.

Close-up of the head. *(Photo: Silkeborg Museum)*

The stubble on Tollund Man's chin and cheeks showed that he had not shaved on his last day alive. *(Photo: Silkeborg Museum)*

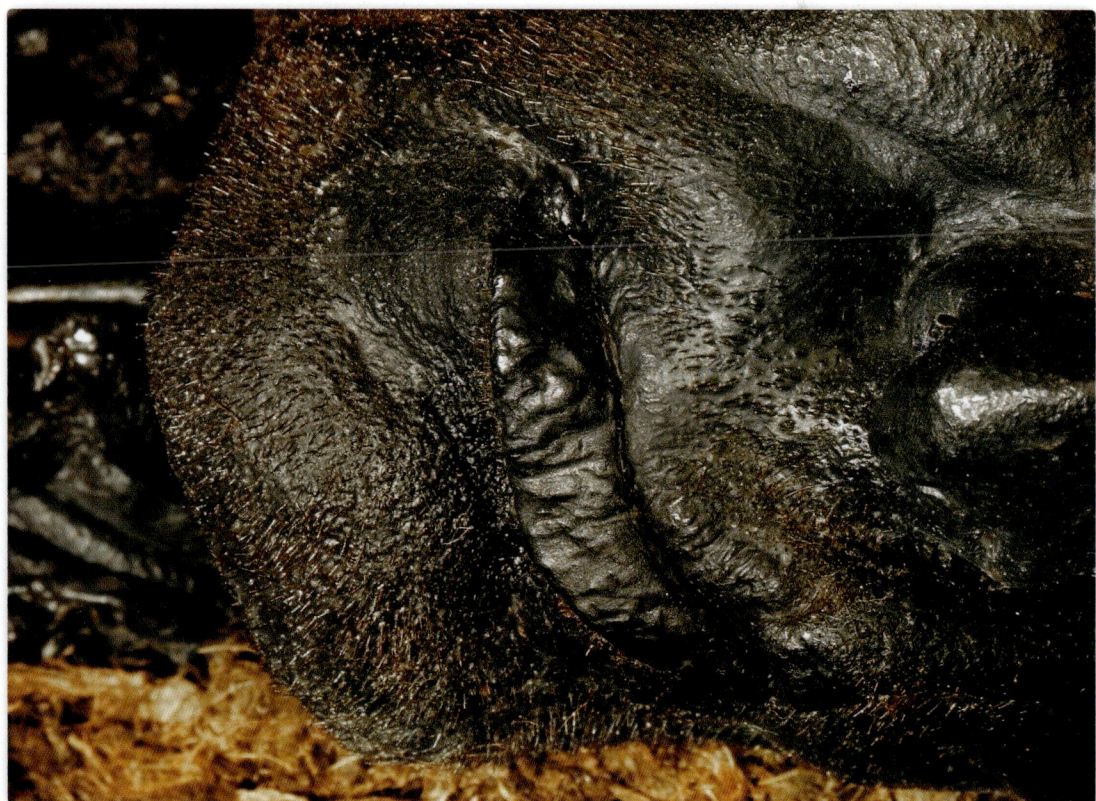

The cap was made from eight pieces of skin sewn together with the hair side turned inwards. *(Photo: Silkeborg Museum)*

Grains and seeds of these plants constituted an important part of the gruel or porridge eaten by Tollund Man between twelve and twenty-four hours before he was hanged. Left: Barley and persicaria. **Right:** Oats. *(Photos: Silkeborg Museum)*

Persicaria. *(Photo: Silkeborg Museum)*

Flax. *(Photo: Silkeborg Museum)*

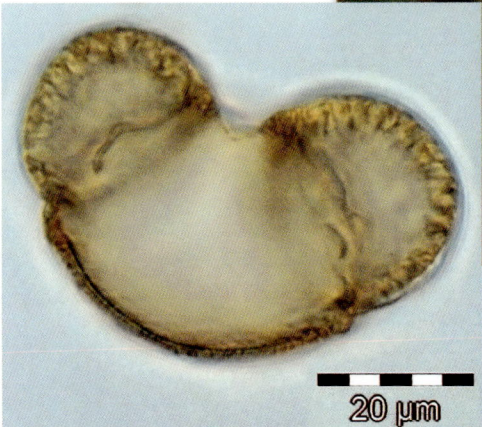

20 μm

Pine pollen. *(Photo: Bent Odgaard)*

Since the Ice Age, Bølling Lake has alternately been a lake, a bog, a meadow, an arable field and now a lake once more. *(Photo: Silkeborg Museum)*

Low winter temperatures are one of the prerequisites for the preservation of a bog body in the wet peat bog. *(Photo: Silkeborg Museum)*

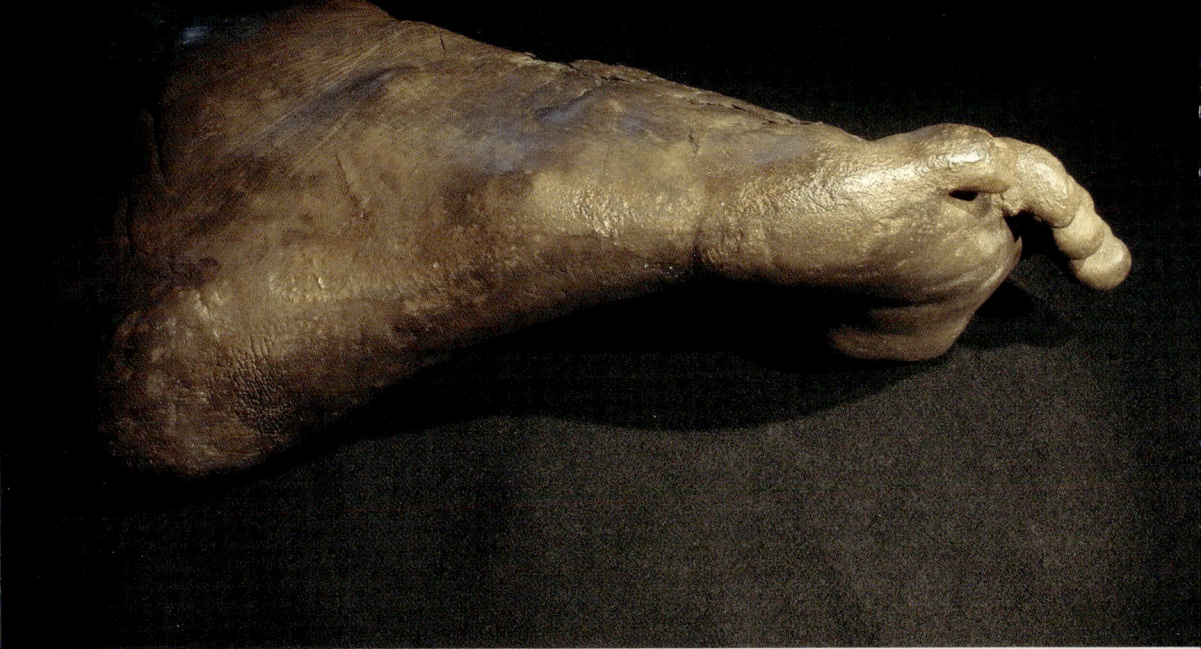

Tollund Man's well-preserved foot after conservation. *(Photo: Silkeborg Museum)*

The pattern on the sole of his right foot comprises two characteristic 'loops'. *(Photo: Silkeborg Museum)*

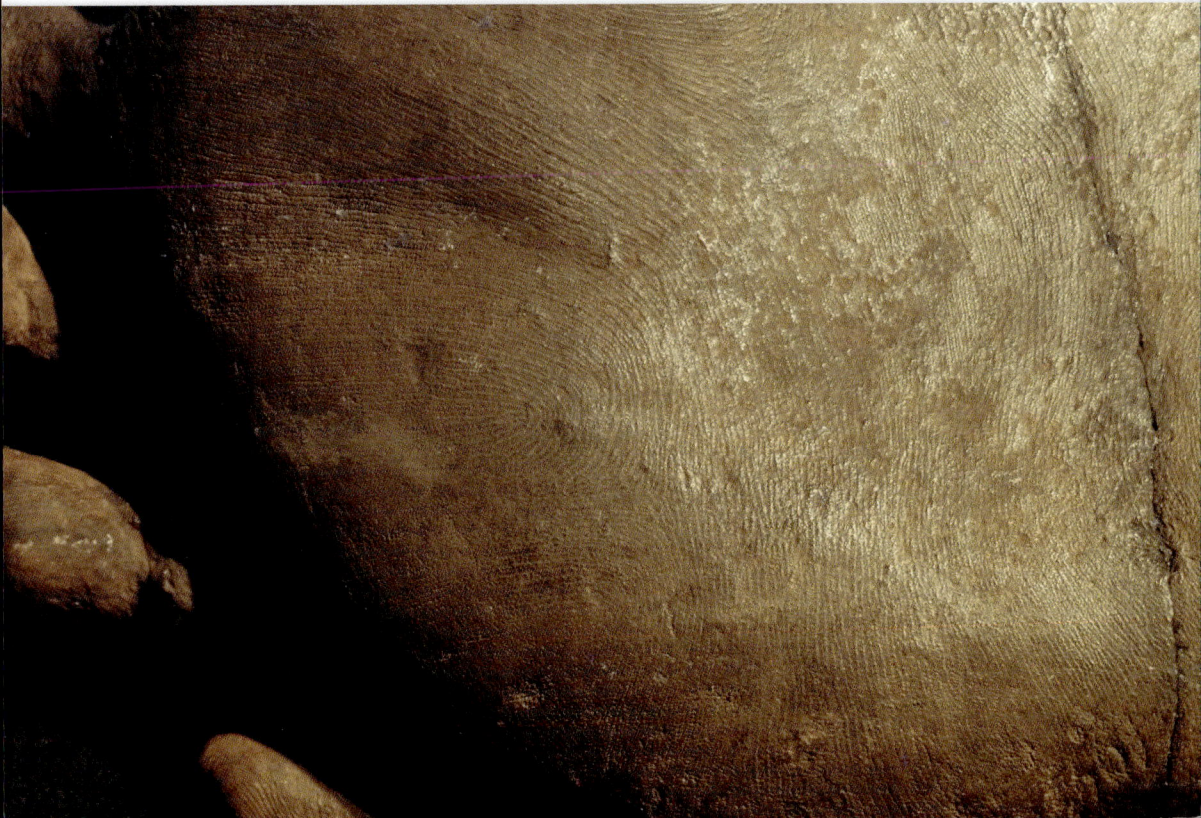

Tollund Man's big toe nail. *(Photo: Silkeborg Museum)*

Tollund Man's right thumb. *(Photo: Silkeborg Museum)*

Right thumb showing a typical arch pattern. *(Photo: Silkeborg Museum)*

Sole of right foot showing scars. *(Photo: Silkeborg Museum)*

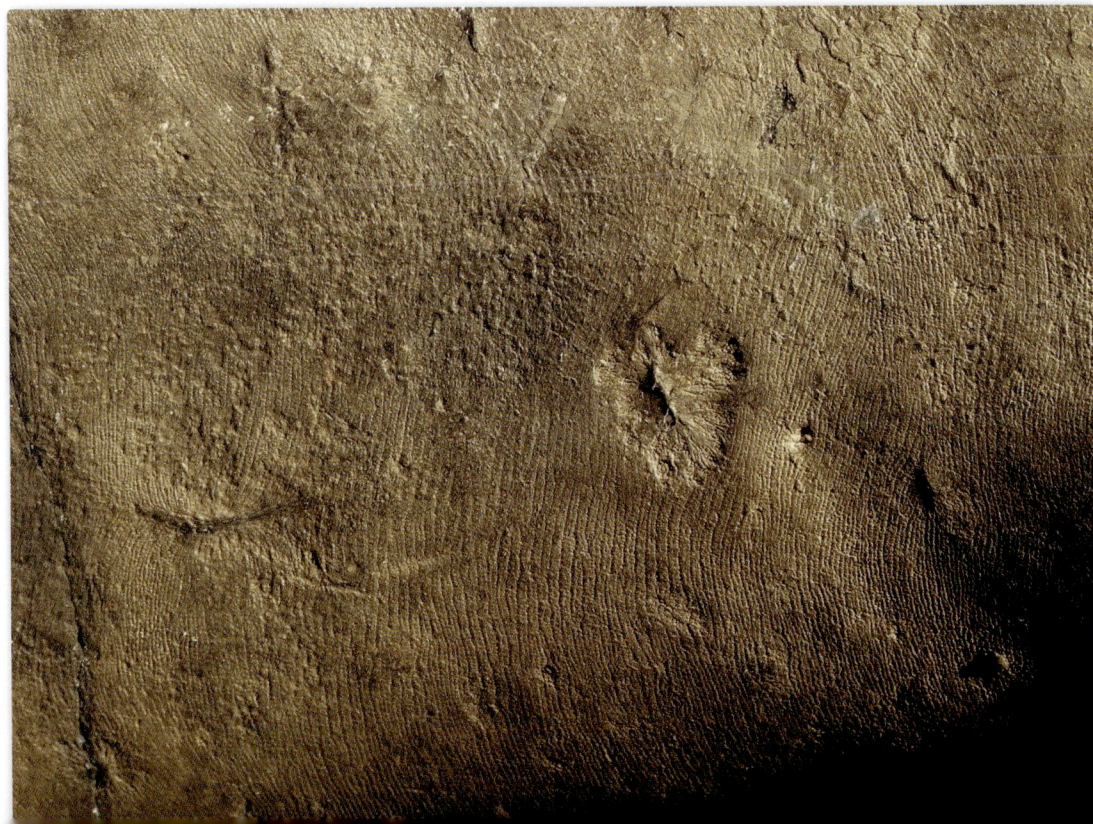

An Iron Age house under construction. *(Reconstruction drawing: Flemming Bau)*

Opposite top: Pottery vessel decorated with fingerprints. *(Photo: Silkeborg Museum)*

Opposite bottom: Lyngsmose. A fortified Iron Age village near Ringkøbing. The defensive ditch can be seen running through the excavated area located in front of the site hut in the centre of the picture. *(Photo: Flyvertaktisk Kommando (Danish Airforce))*

The house as archaeologists find it today. *(Reconstruction drawing: Flemming Bau)*

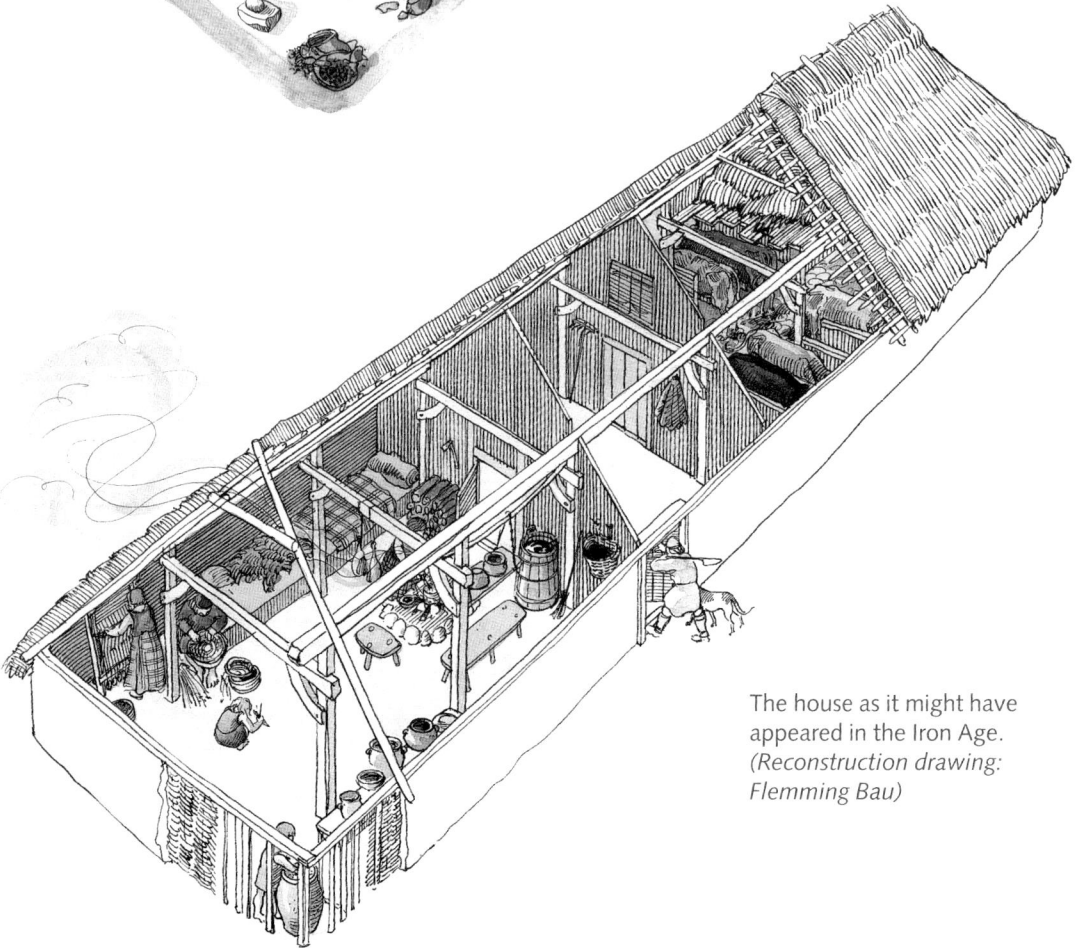

The house as it might have appeared in the Iron Age. *(Reconstruction drawing: Flemming Bau)*

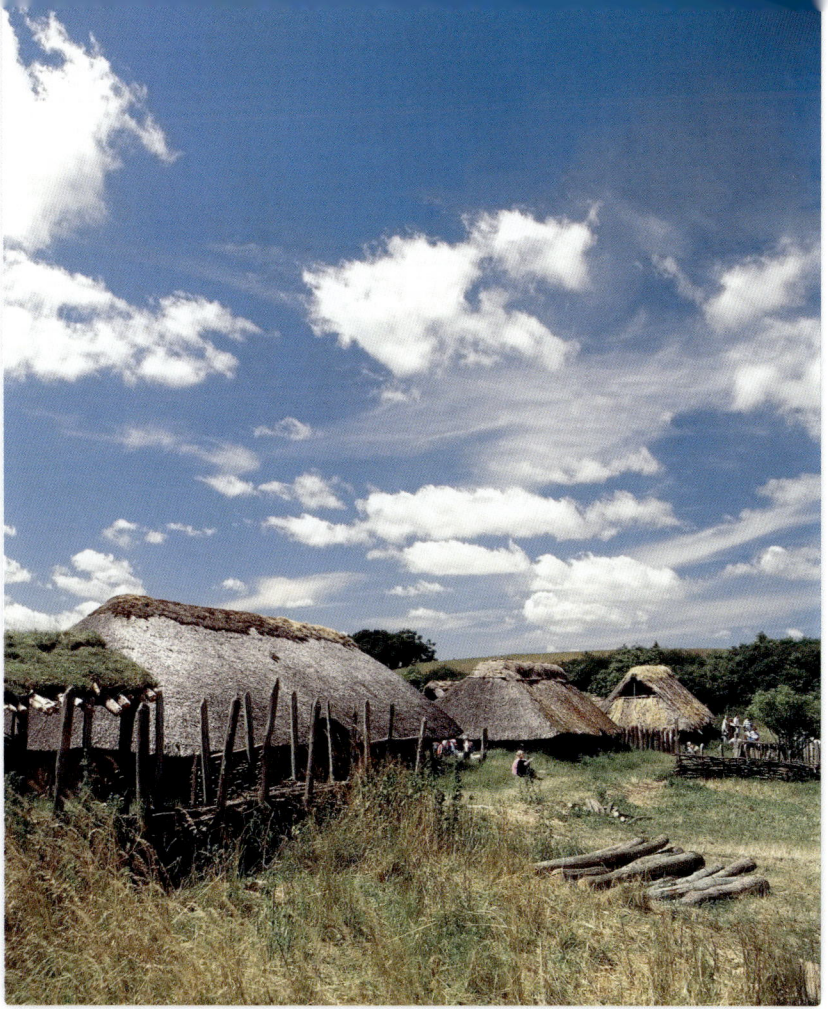

Reconstructed Iron Age village. *(Photo: Lejre Land of Legends)*

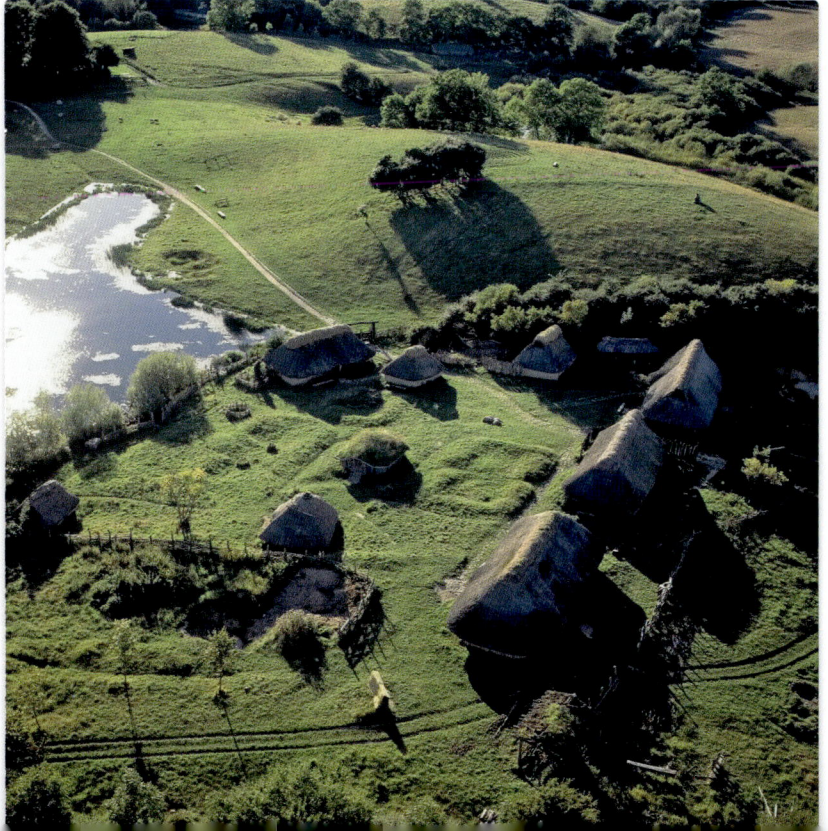

Reconstruction of an Iron Age village excavated at Grønbjerg in Western Jutland. *(Photo: Lejre Land of Legends)*

Life inside an Iron Age house. *(Photo: Lejre Land of Legends)*

The potsherds from the kiln at Gjern were patiently reassembled to give about fifty whole vessels, out of the sixty estimated to be present. *(Photo: Silkeborg Museum)*

Hvinningdal near Silkeborg. Burials from the Early Iron Age had been placed around a barrow from the Late Neolithic. They are covered with circular stone pavements. *(Photo: Silkeborg Museum)*

The circular stone pavements may cover several burials, which are evident as small dark patches. They contain ash and remains of bones from the funeral pyre. Perhaps this was a family cemetery. *(Photo: Silkeborg Museum)*

Iron smelting. *(Reconstruction drawing: Flemming Bau)*

Tollund Man's attitude in the peat was not just the result of a casual 'dumping' of the body, but its careful arrangement in a 'sleeping position': His mouth and eyes have been gently closed by those left behind. *(Photo: Robert Clark)*

A bracteate is a circular gold pendant with a suspension lug; it most commonly bears a religious motif. This example shows a scene which must depict Odin's magical blowing in the ear of Balder's horse to cure its lameness. The bracteate dates from about AD 400 and reveals a detailed knowledge of the Ase religion. *(Photo: Bent Lange)*

The Gundestrup Cauldron comprising 9kg of embossed silver. Probably manufactured in the vicinity of the Black Sea. Used as an offering in Rævemosen in Himmerland. The figures on the vessel depict parts of Celtic mythology. *(Photo: The National Museum)*

The most exact dating method for wood is dendrochronology. For this to be applied the sample material must generally be of oak and contain a large number of tree rings. The width of the rings varies according to good, normal or poor years of growth, forming a distinctive pattern. Given access to a local tree-ring chronology, with a calendar date for its beginning and for its end, it is possible, by measuring the width of the tree rings in the sample material, and with the aid of a computer programme, to match the pattern of sample to the chronology and thereby find the exact date of the sample.

The post was analysed and expectations were high, but it could not be dated – the oak wood used as timber had grown abnormally and the uncertainty was too great. When an opportunity arose to have the sample radiocarbon dated, the museum immediately responded in the affirmative. The dating procedure was

The post from the wooden road which still lay in Tobias Lassen's woodshed. Radiocarbon dating of the post revealed that the road dated back to, or was in use, as early as the Late Bronze Age. *(Photo: Silkeborg Museum)*

carried out in The Netherlands where a project was in progress aimed at dating a number of bog bodies from North-West Europe.

Shortly afterwards the museum received a letter from The Netherlands in which an apology was given for a possible error in the date they had obtained; they believed it was too old. But to the great joy of the museum it revealed that the post was from a tree felled and used for building the bridge/road in 700–600 BC. The post is, accordingly, a couple of centuries older than Tollund Man and Elling Woman. The fact that the road could have functioned for a long time after it was built seems highly likely, taking into account the fact that the posts remained

Wooden corduroy road from the Iron Age excavated in the bog Speghøje Mose, west of Bjældskovdal. (Photo: Silkeborg Museum)

so well preserved that they could be pulled up and used for fuel by twentieth-century peat cutters. Archaeological records of roads reveal that they most often continued in use for very long periods of time – in some cases 1,000 years – and were repeatedly repaired.

A conservative reconstruction of the scenario in Bjældskovdal in the Early Iron Age could be that peat was cut alongside a road running across the bog. Corpses were placed in three of the peat cuttings and were subsequently converted by nature into bog bodies. The corpses were – at least in the cases of Tollund Man and Elling Woman – of people who had been killed by hanging, after which they were carried down the wooden road, out into the bog, and deposited in a peat cutting. On these occasions the road served a cultic purpose, whereas it was normally employed for everyday activities.

ON THE WRONG TRACK

As a result of this information, yet another bog body became involved into the museum's detailed investigations. Some way to the north of Bjældskovdal, about 6km away, a bog body was found near the Hærvej in 1898. It was in the bog Kragelund Fattiggårdens Mose at Nedre Frederiks and the body was that of a man. It was well preserved and clad in a form of tunic. On his feet the man had leather boots. A stake lay nearby and he had clearly been buried in a hole cut down through the peat. The discovery was thoroughly investigated by the National Museum, from where it since has disappeared, but the clothing and the boots remain in the museum's collections. Photographs were taken, and this was probably one of the first times in Denmark that this invention was applied with the primary intention of recording an archaeological find at the site where it was discovered.

In 1998, the National Museum had the clothing radiocarbon dated. This revealed that it was from about AD 1045–1145, corresponding well to the cut of the garment. This was the body of a Viking or perhaps someone from the Early Middle Ages who, for some inexplicable reason, had died on the spot or somewhere close by, and who had then been buried in the raised bog – a natural death while on the road, the victim of a murder or someone fleeing from the battle at Grathe Hede in 1157?

The date reveals this example to be isolated in time because most bog bodies are from the Early Iron Age. Consequently, Nedre Frederiks Man is the exception that proves the rule. Corresponding examples are known from Sweden, for instance

The bog body from the Viking Age or Early Middle Ages found on the morning of 25 May 1898 in Fattiggårdens Mose near Nedre Frederiks Mose, a short distance north of Bjældskovdal. *(Photo: The National Museum)*

Bocksten Man; a bog body found near Varberg, which is of even later date – fourteenth century. It is thought that he was a victim of the wars which took place between Sweden and Denmark at that time. His corpse was secured to the bottom of the bog by having a stake hammered through it.

The two men have in common the fact that they date from a Christian period and it is therefore difficult to see them as the victims of a pagan cult. This could, on the other hand, be a possible explanation for the fate of Tollund Man and Elling Woman.

6

THE REDISCOVERED CORPSE

Museum visitors admired Tollund Man's well-preserved head and sometimes asked cautiously about the rest of his body.

The pressure mounted as a consequence of Glob's book *The Bog People*, words such as scandal were employed, and I had a personal interest in finding an explanation so there was really no alternative. At the National Museum there was nothing in writing about the detached body. Nowhere was there a mention of archive or storage. At Silkeborg Museum, Tollund Man is recorded as no. 202/1950 – a number which was added to his display case in indelible ink, should anyone be in any doubt.

The National Museum's Conservation Department turned out to have two jars in which his feet were preserved. One of them was, however, in a poor state as the preservation fluid had evaporated at some point; there was also the well-preserved thumb and the big toe. Silkeborg Museum asked for these body parts to be returned, and this request was granted with the exception of the toe, which has never turned up. Shortly afterwards, one of the National Museum's curators telephoned to say that 'something' had been found on a shelf in the stores which, judging from its appearance, could be Tollund Man's torso. This now completely desiccated item was also transferred to Silkeborg – the soft tissues, especially the skin, had with time acquired a consistency like that of thick leather; the chest was the best preserved part.

Some months would elapse before Silkeborg Museum received an anonymous hint: try asking the Normal-Anatomical Institute about the remainder of the body. Here, true enough, were – more or less – the missing bits of Tollund Man, however with the crucial difference that only the bones were preserved. As can be read in the report on the bog body from Søgårds Mose in 1942 (Daugbjerg Man), it was normal practice at the National Museum to clean the bones of bog bodies of any soft tissues before, in the form of a skeleton, these were handed over to the Normal-Anatomical Institute.

Tollund Man's bones were now, in principle, all assembled, and Silkeborg Museum was now in possession of the well-preserved head, a well-preserved right foot (though lacking the big toe), the thumb of the right hand, a less well-preserved left foot and a torso with desiccated soft tissues; the remainder of the body was present in skeletal form. In order to complete the picture, Silkeborg Museum was contacted shortly afterwards by Moesgård Museum and asked if a jam jar marked 'Tollund Man's gut contents' could be collected. The whole case has many elements which, according to temperament, one can either laugh or cry about. It should, however, be seen in the light of the situation in post-war years, when possibilities for conservation were limited, when a certain dialogue prevailed between the National Museum and the amateurs of provincial museums and when the ethical attitude of the time to the exhibition of corpses was very different. Display to the public was out of the question, especially if bodies were well preserved – they should preferably be hidden away and, in the case of Tollund Man, ideally be forgotten altogether.

New perspectives now opened up – the possibility of new investigations and also of recreating the sight which met the Højgaard family on 6 May 1950 – Tollund Man as he lay in the bog.

The investigation which was easiest to carry out was, as already mentioned, radiocarbon dating. Once cleaned of store-room dust and other contaminating materials from the bog's encapsulating layers, this revealed that Tollund Man died in about 220 BC. The sample was taken from the desiccated skin of his chest and must give the time of his death. Samples from other parts of his body, where cell replacement is slower or virtually non-existent, would have given a date corresponding to his childhood. His thumb, with the beautifully rounded nail, was so well preserved that its fingerprint could be seen with the naked eye. Well aware that there are no records from the Early Iron Age which could reveal his identity it was, even so, with some excitement that a high-power photograph of the fingerprint was handed over to the CID in Silkeborg in 1978. They, in turn, sent it on to the Central Bureau for Identification where AC H.P. Andersson took care of the matter; a picture of the sole of the right foot was also included. After examining the material, he wrote:

> On the photograph of the right thumb, a typical arch pattern can be seen. This type
> of pattern is commonly found on the prints which are taken today and its location on

the right thumb occurs in rather more than 2% of the fingerprint forms held in the Danish Police's fingerprint records.

On the base area (behind the toes) on the sole of the right foot, 2 loops can be seen, which is a frequently occurring pattern distribution, also in modern times (the undersigned has the same distribution).

Behind the base area there are two scars: The upper one appears as a scar from a cut, the lower as a stab wound.

As the skin surfaces visible on the photographs are, as mentioned, presumably the corium/derma, it is not possible to express an opinion with respect to the degree to which the epidermis may be worn, and for the same reasons it is difficult to provide any information with respect to whether the foot in life had worn shoes.

Andersson's observation that it is the corium/derma which is present, and not the epidermis, means that the statements of former times about people subsequently found as bog bodies apparently having had a special status before their death and not being involved in hard labour can no longer be taken seriously. The deceased's epidermis must have dissolved long ago during the long time it spent in wet conditions. Anyone who has ever had their hands in water for any period of time will know that the hard skin falls off and leaves the underlying corium/derma.

Perhaps his fingerprints will, even so, at some time in the future give us a lead as to where he lived while he was alive. Who knows whether one day we might find a potsherd on which there is a fingerprint which matches that of Tollund Man? Fingerprints were a favourite decoration on pots from his time.

The fact that there are two scars on the sole of his foot need not necessarily mean that he had been subjected to violence; the most obvious explanation is that in life, while barefoot, he had stood on some sharp object such as a stone. However, if the imagination is allowed to run riot, then there could be another explanation:

Both to the north, i.e. in Borremose in Himmerland, and to the west, for example at Lyngsmose near Ringkøbing, agricultural settlements have been found dating from the Celtic Iron Age – the time of the bog bodies – which were surrounded by defensive structures such as banks and ditches. These low ditches do not, on the face of it, appear as if they would be difficult to take by storm. However, some devilish devices have been discovered on the bases and the sides of these ditches – Iron Age land mines! The ditches were covered with thousands of small vertical pointed stakes intended to hinder an attack on the village. They were well hidden under the shallow water in the ditch. Outside the ditch there were further rows and rows of stakes, set in circular pits and covered with loose material which gave away when someone trod on it, impaling their foot on the point.

Could Tollund Man have trodden on one of these stakes and thereby injured and infected his foot? The Romans referred to these pointed stakes as 'Caesar's Lilies', and they formed part of the sophisticated defences which surrounded Roman citadels.

Previously inexplicable broad belts found at other Iron Age villages, apparent as hundreds of black patches in the soil, could now be explained by the fact that they had once contained these now vanished 'lilies'. Only in the most fortunate circumstances, at places such as Lyngsmose where the dampness of the soil has preserved the wood, are they now to be found.

The base of the ditch showing the sharp wooden spikes ('Caesar's Lilies'). *(Photo: Palle Eriksen)*

In the 1960s, the author excavated just such a broad belt of closely-spaced black patches. In the evenings, on the television news, it could be seen how the Vietcong guerrillas in Vietnam prevented modern American paratroopers from landing by placing dense rows of bamboo canes in the ground with sharpened points upwards. The black patches and the subject of the television news story had much in common: I could just not see it at the time.

THE RE-ASSEMBLED TOLLUND MAN

Once virtually all the parts of Tollund Man had been relocated and taken to Silkeborg, the thought occurred of whether it was possible to remedy the decision which today must be seen as a mistake: only to have conserved the head and to have allowed the rest of the body to dry out.

The idea was to show the museum's visitors how Tollund Man had looked when he was found in 1950 – a spectacle which was now no longer considered 'macabre'.

The problem was of course that it was extremely difficult to re-assemble the body parts, given their very different states of preservation – the incredibly well-preserved head joined together with the desiccated torso and the limbs which existed only as bones. The idea was impossible for both aesthetic and ethical reasons.

A suggestion came from conservators that the dehydrated torso could perhaps be re-hydrated and restored to the form it had in 1950, likewise the distorted bones. But the soft tissues which, in the name of science, had been removed from the latter could not be recreated. Then there were the two feet, of which one was very well preserved while the other was in a very poor and twisted state.

Many sleepless nights gave time for reflection and brought certainty with respect to the impossibility of such a solution. Scientifically, it would not yield anything new – the documentation of Tollund Man's appearance took place already in 1950, and new discoveries would then only be based on a reconstructed state: DNA analyses, the application of new medical advances and improved dating methods would be rendered impossible if the dehydrated tissues were treated chemically. The dehydrated, un-conserved parts represent a veritable gold mine with respect to future research into life in the Iron Age. Destruction of this potential in order to provide visitors with the opportunity of seeing Tollund Man more or less as he appeared when he was discovered was too high a price to pay.

The ethical aspect had also to be taken into consideration, and whether this question has yet been satisfactorily resolved is still a source of some doubt to me. Throughout my life as an archaeologist the investigation of graves containing more or less well-preserved skeletons has been an everyday activity. For many years, skeletons had in my eyes a status on a par with flint axes – purely scientific objects – nothing more, nothing less.

My attitude changed one day when I was excavating a child's grave dating from the first century AD. Any remains of the deceased had disappeared completely, but in the grave were small pots containing food and drink, placed there for the journey to the Kingdom of the Dead, which it was imagined the child was about to embark upon. Small ornaments had also been attached to the child's clothes. Judging from the size of the grave, the child was the same age as my own child. Suddenly, I could sense what a terrible grief the parents must have endured on the child's death. That grave became not just a discovery of scientific interest, but also something of great significance for my own respect for what the dead child represented.

One solution to the whole conundrum could be a very detailed recreation of the body as it had appeared on excavation at the National Museum in 1950. This would be possible on the basis of photographs and the surviving dehydrated parts.

Experts able to produce such a reconstruction were to be found at the Natural History Museum in Aarhus. They had experience of casting techniques and modelling. However, Silkeborg Museum wanted to see the result before it was presented to the public. When the reconstruction was finished, it was to be carefully evaluated aesthetically and ethically. The possibility that the reconstruction could be rejected was a real one and this situation did not change when the story prematurely reached the press.

Ultimately, Tollund Man's reconstructed body was attached to his well-preserved head and among the first to see the result were the Højgaard family, who had discovered him. They were in no doubt – it was him they had found.

The decision to exhibit Tollund Man as a 'complete' figure was taken with the option in mind that, should perceptions of the aesthetic and ethical aspects of this exhibition change, it would be unproblematic to return to the situation prior to reconstruction of the body.

'Tollund Man to be admitted to hospital', was the headline in several Danish newspapers and both domestic and foreign television channels showed great interest. It happened one Saturday in 2002, at Aarhus University Hospital's

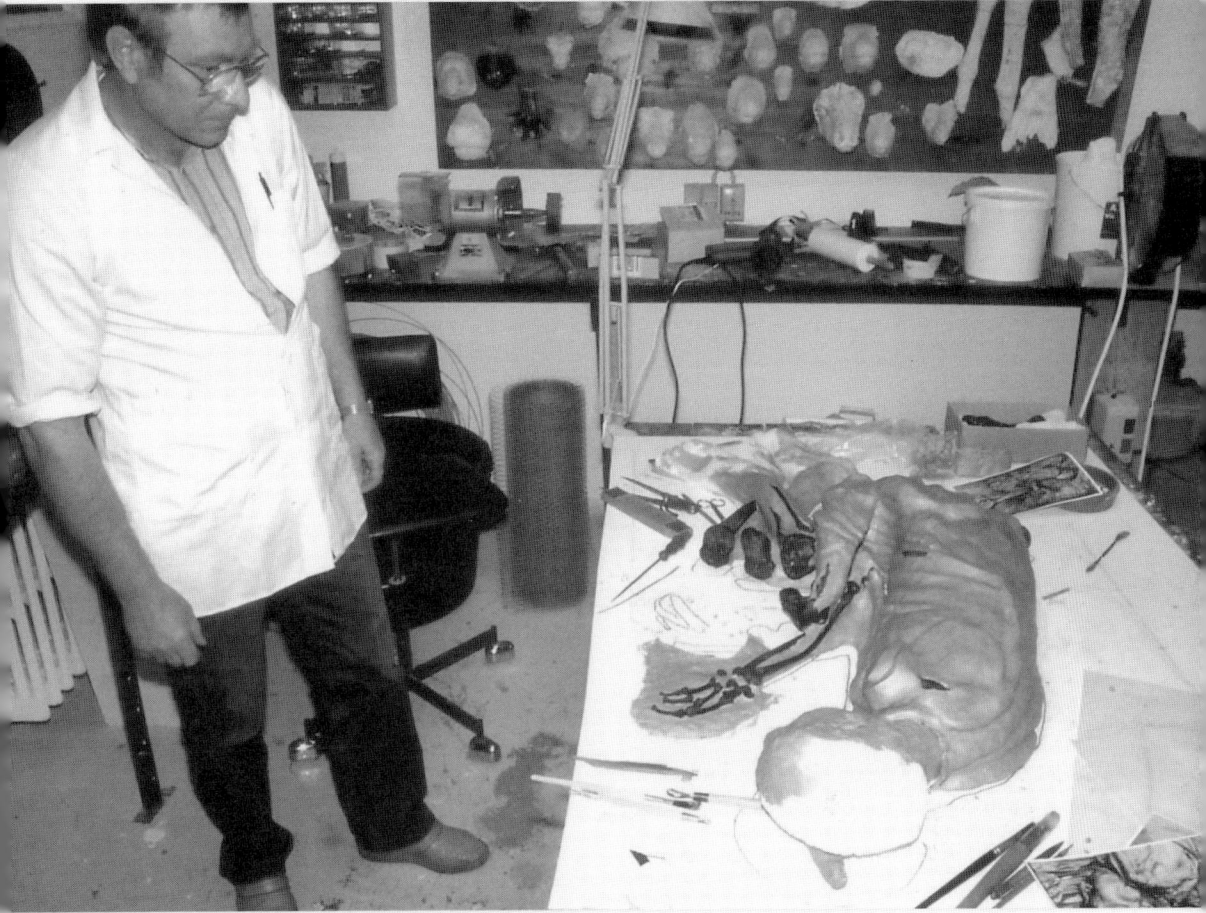

The Natural History Museum's reconstruction of Tollund Man's body. Conservator Lars Bo Nielsen is working on the reconstruction. *(Photo: The Natural History Museum)*

Radiology Department and the Institute of Forensic Medicine, to allow new technology, CT-scanning, to provide new information.

The journey from Silkeborg to the University Hospital in Aarhus took place under police escort. Tollund Man was now regarded as a national treasure and it was important therefore that he should ideally complete the return trip unscathed; it was very different from his first journey on a horse and cart and as unaccompanied freight with the State Railways.

The initiative for this piece of research came from the same group of doctors and dentists who, a short time before, had carried out a thorough re-examination of Grauballe Man.

A police escort with blue flashing lights secured the transfer of Tollund Man to the University Hospital in Aarhus. *(Photo: Taken directly from the television screen)*

The actual examination of Tollund Man only took a day and resulted in about 16,000 digital images, after which he was allowed home again.

A dose of x-rays corresponding to that used in this case could not of course be applied to a living person, but for a long-dead bog body it was quite another matter.

The many images are available to science, and will continue to be in the future. They mean that new investigations can take place in coming years without requiring the presence of the actual body. Should the improbable happen that, in some way or other, the bog body becomes damaged or disappears, it has now been recorded in minute detail.

With the most recent CT-scanning technique it is also possible to see soft tissues which previously could only have been investigated via an autopsy. Tollund Man's tongue had never been seen before and this was found to be swollen, as is the case when someone has been hanged.

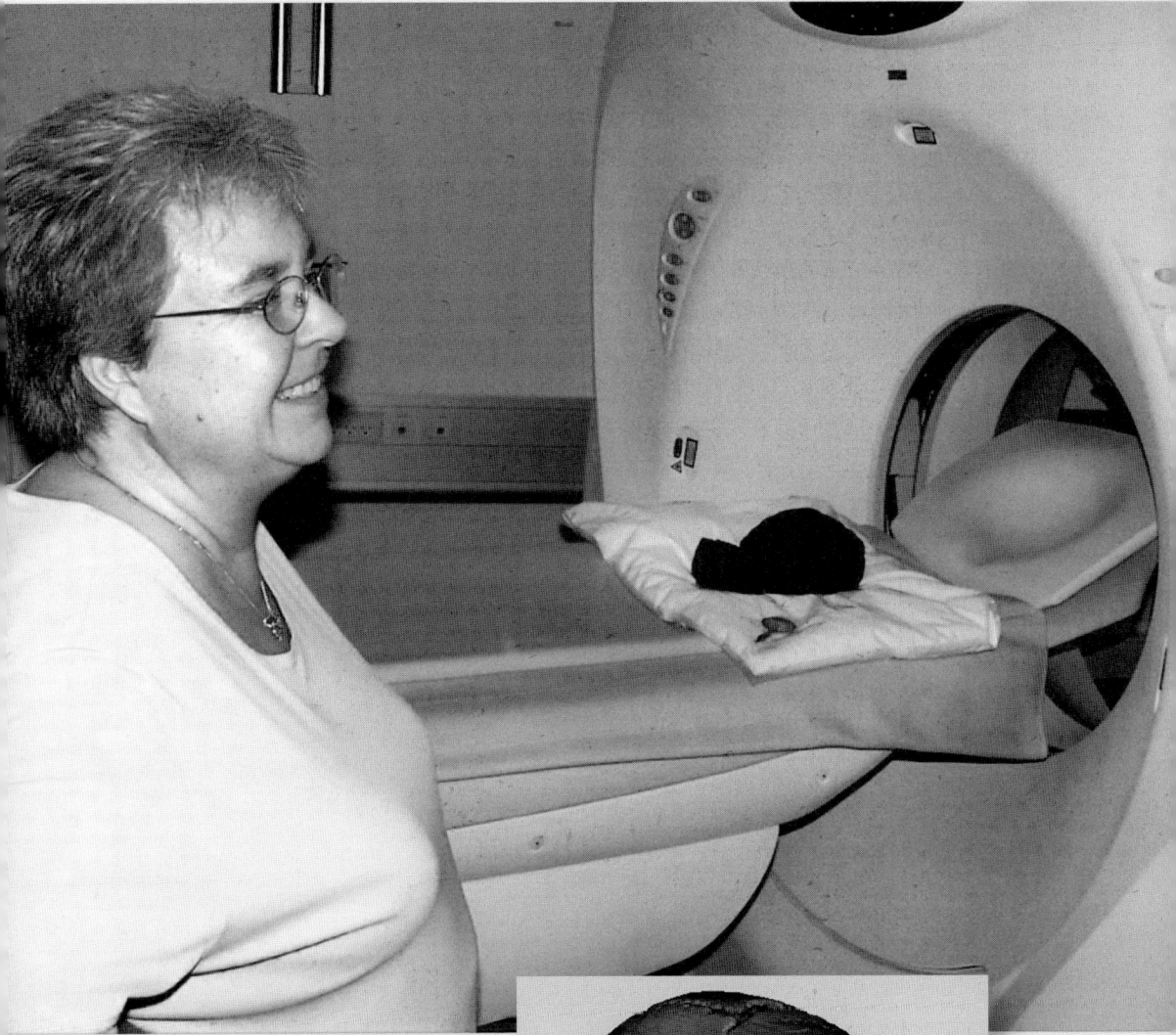

Tollund Man's head on its way into
the CT-scanner.

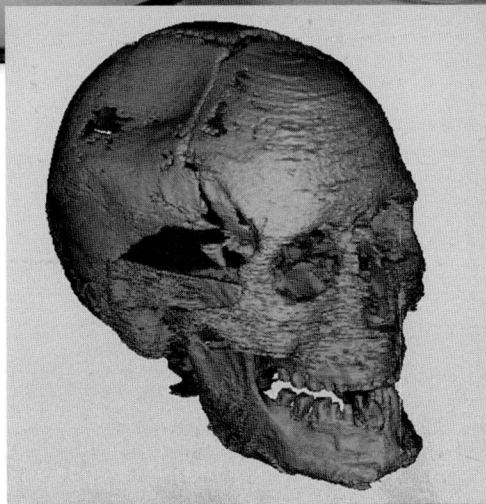

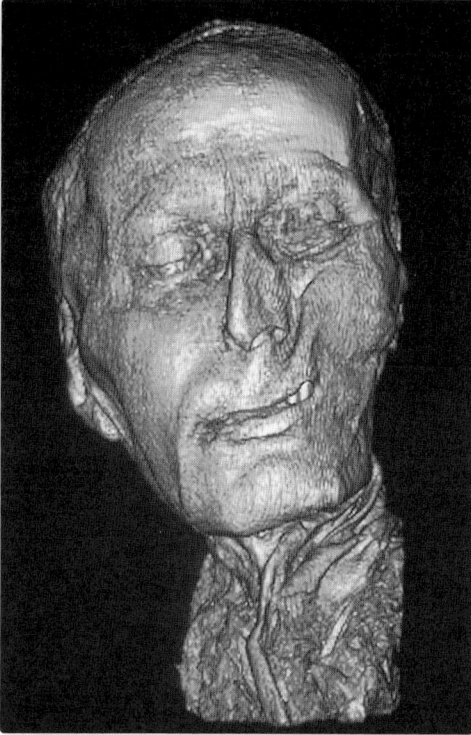

Computer-enhanced x-rays of Tollund
Man's head. *(Photo: Silkeborg Museum)*

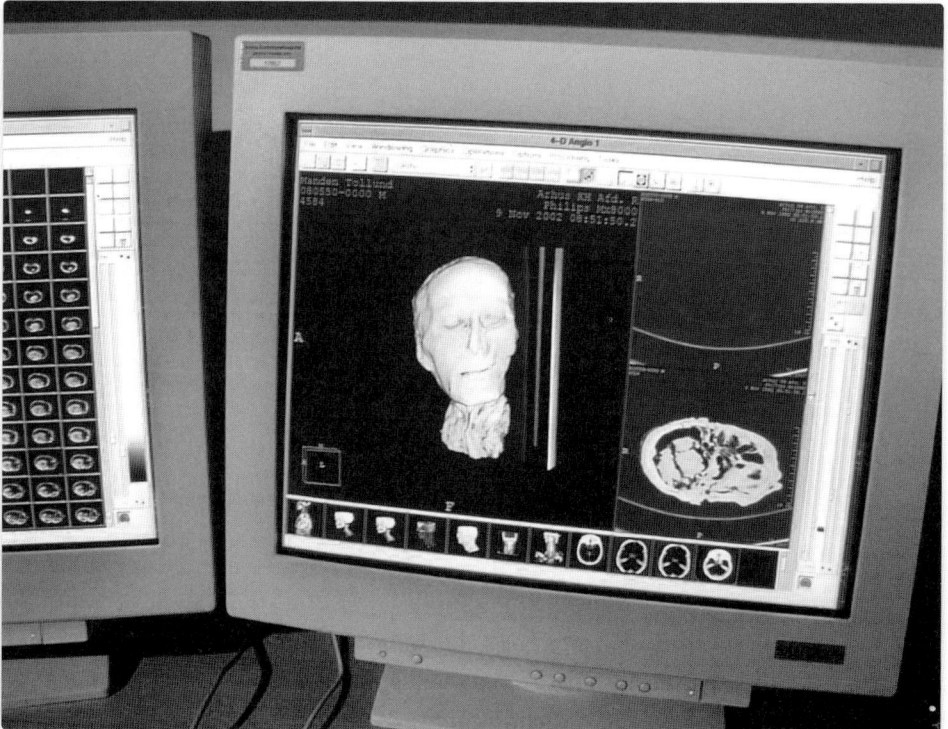

Consultant Ulrik
Pedersen performing
fibre endoscopy of the
brain via the spinal
canal. *(Photo: Silkeborg
Museum)*

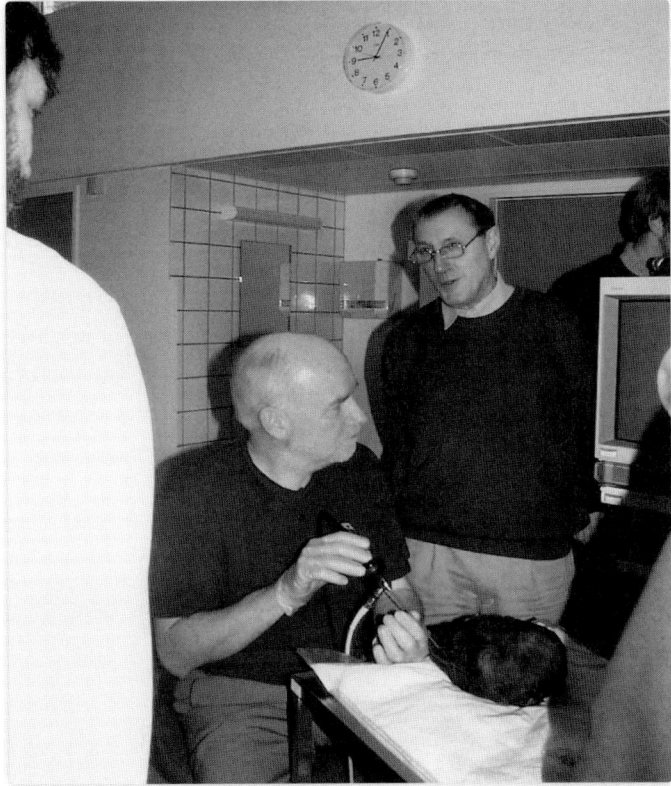

It was hoped that DNA analysis of the bog bodies could potentially provide information on genetic origins and hereditary illnesses. For example, were Tollund Man and Elling Woman closely related? However, it has unfortunately become apparent that it is not yet possible, given existing techniques, to perform such analyses on a bog body, because the DNA does not survive in the bog's acidic water. It may be achievable in future years, perhaps using a sample drilled out from the middle of a preserved tooth.

Hair was taken for analysis because diet is reflected in its mineral composition. A sufficiently long hair can provide an extended account of Iron Age dietary preferences, seen over a longer period than the twelve to twenty-four hours which could be read from Tollund Man's stomach contents.

The great surprise in the investigations was that it proved possible, via the spinal canal, to push an endoscope up to Tollund Man's brain, and this was found to be exceptionally well preserved. 'But we are unlikely ever to discover what he thought at the moment of his death,' observed pathologist Professor Markil Gregersen dryly.

To which another physician retorted: 'We never know what research will bring!' The headline on Danish TV-2's news bulletin that evening was: 'Silkeborg has the world's best brain!'

The new data also included the information that Tollund Man's teeth were all intact, although one was skew and a finger bone showed signs of a heeled fracture.

A more detailed analysis of Elling Woman was also carried out at Silkeborg Museum and revealed the presence of intact nits (lice eggs).

Tollund Man's skin has been examined under infrared light for any traces of tattoos on his head and torso. The result was negative, but it is possible that any tattoos present were just not visible using current technology. Tattoos were probably a very widespread phenomenon in prehistory. The body of Ötzi, the well-preserved 5,000-year-old Iceman from Tyrol, was extensively decorated in this way.

7

OTHER BOG BODIES

We can now turn our attention to a number of other bog bodies dated to the end of the Bronze Age and to the Celtic Iron Age. These examples have been chosen because the circumstances of their discovery are well documented and their state of preservation is good enough to enable details with respect to cause of death, sex and age, clothing etc. to be deduced.

HARALDSKÆR WOMAN (QUEEN GUNHILD), 1835

This woman's body was found in a bog near Vejle in 1835 and was the first bog body to be perceived by archaeology as an anonymous prehistoric individual. Immediately following its discovery, and because Haraldskær lies so close to Jelling, the corpse was given the 'honour' of being identified as the Norwegian king Eric Bloodaxe's queen, Gunhild, whose reputation as an imperious woman of easy virtue prompted King Harald Bluetooth to entice her into an ambush and drown her in the morass.

This thrilling explanation was soundly discredited by the twenty-two-year-old archaeologist J.J.A. Worsaae who arrived at a correct scientific understanding of this and other corpses from the bogs: he maintained that the great majority of them must date from prehistory. Subsequently, his interpretation has stood unchallenged. Worsaae's interpretation was a very brave undertaking as King Frederick VI had personally donated an oak-wood coffin for the 'queen'. To this very day she still rests in her sarcophagus in St Nicholas' Church in Vejle. The items discovered with her, a skin cape, hairnet and sticks (with which it is assumed she was secured to the bottom of the bog), were all sent to Copenhagen.

In 1978 the corpse was examined by the same team of doctors and dental experts who examined Tollund Man and Elling Woman. The conclusion they reached was

Haraldskær Woman ('Queen Gunhild') in her sarcophagus in St Nicholas' Church in Vejle. *(Photo: Silkeborg Museum)*

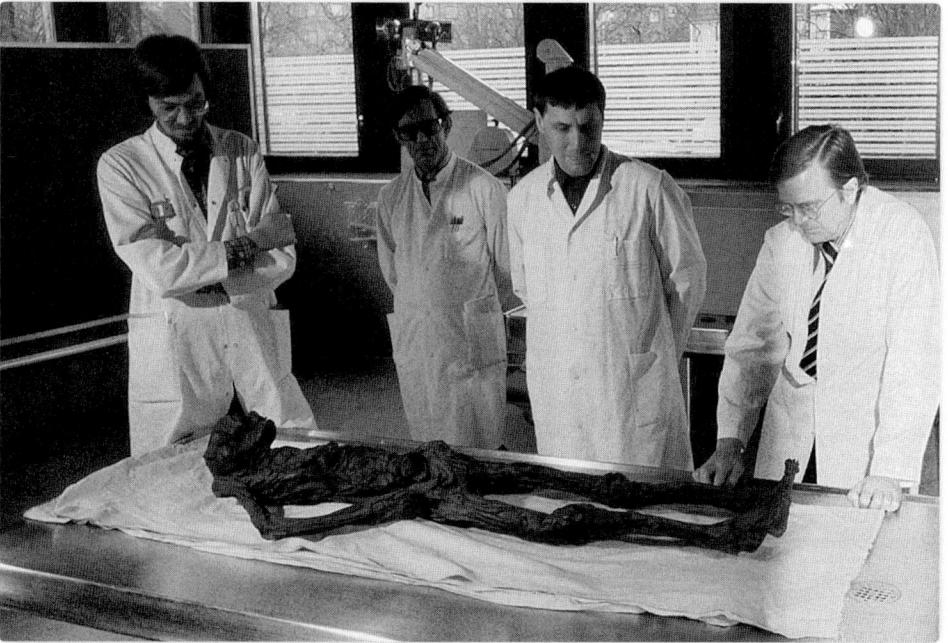

Haraldskær Woman on the dissecting table in 1978. The examination was carried out by pathologist Markil Gregersen, radiologist Bent Langfelt and dentist H.P. Philipsen. *(Photo: Silkeborg Museum)*

that she had died at the age of about forty and was of modest height, about 150cm. However, when found, she was only about 133cm tall. On the basis of pressure marks and the presence of crooks made from tree branches it seems she was secured to the bottom of the bog: a stick over each knee and one over each elbow, as well as over her chest and belly. An actual cause of death could not be determined.

'Queen Gunhild' was subsequently radiocarbon dated to about 200 BC, i.e. the Celtic Iron Age – the time of the bog bodies.

THE STIDSHOLT HEAD, 1859

One day, on the border between the two districts of Dronninglund and Horne, a boy pushed a stick down next to a cloth band sticking up from a meadow – and out popped a head.

The authorities, including general practitioner Jacobi in Sæby, who described the find, report that the head had been severed from the body by a sharp blow from back to front. The blow had been directed such that it struck the fourth and the front part of the third cervical vertebra and then continued obliquely through the neck, cutting the neck muscles and ripping off a piece of skin beneath the chin.

Most of the teeth were in situ, although some had been knocked out by the boy's stick. However, the 'incisors and canines' of the upper jaw were missing, a point which Jacobi found strange. Jacobi writes that the lower teeth are worn and that they had met the upper teeth in a way similar to that seen in Eskimos.

A woven hair band, of almost a metre in length and with fringes, was bound in the hair.

There are several examples of severed heads, with no accompanying bodies, having been deposited in bogs, for example at Roum and at Osterby in Northern Schleswig. This brings to mind the Celtic culture in which severed heads were involved in cult activities.

As with the head from Roum, dealt with below, the Stidsholt Head is presumed to be that of a woman, because the long hair is piled into a 'beehive' hairstyle and the face shows no sign of beard growth. The severed head from Osterby in Northern Schleswig has a male hairstyle, a so-called Swabian knot. Osterby Man is dated to the first century AD.

The head from the bog Stidsholt Mose is kept at the National Museum in Copenhagen. A radiocarbon date was obtained of around 300 BC.

THE BODY FROM KROGENS MØLLEMOSE, 1878

The site lies in Torslev parish in the vicinity of Dronninglund and the bog body was found during peat cutting at a depth of about 1m. The peat cutters caught sight of some skin and when they pulled on it, a number of human bones were revealed. The corpse is assumed to have lain outstretched with its head to the west. Either on the body itself or directly beside it lay a hooded skin cape.

There was also a leather ring, 47cm long and 1cm wide. This was bound together with a plaited leather cord made from four thin thongs. According to the report from 1878 it was thought that this could have been used as a collar for a large dog, but a more likely explanation is that it was the hangman's noose.

Many textile fragments were associated with the body, including possible remains of a cloth bag. During the excavation it proved impossible to recover all parts of these as several pieces of cloth fell back into the water together with three skin fragments, possibly from a further cape!

The corpse was not examined in further detail and the sex has therefore not been determined. It was, however, assumed from the delicate bones of the corpse that it was a woman.

The body from Krogens Møllemose has been radiocarbon dated to around 300 BC, i.e. the middle of the Celtic Iron Age.

HULDREMOSE WOMAN, 1879

This corpse, found in the bog Huldremose on Djursland, is perhaps the bog body which, at the time of its discovery, remained in the best state of preservation. It also very impressively 'survived' being placed in a coffin and reburied in Ørum churchyard before subsequently being exhumed and sent to the Museum of Northern Antiquities in Copenhagen, where the enthusiasm it prompted was no greater than that in 1904 and reburial in a churchyard was again considered.

The fantastically well-preserved clothes were taken from the body, rinsed in water and hung to dry. The first impression was that this was the body of a man who had disappeared from the district about six to seven years previously. This was later discounted. The man, however, never did turn up.

On the upper part of the body, which proved to be that of a woman, there were two skin capes, one on top of the other – the innermost with the hair side inwards, the outer, a magnificent garment, with the hair side turned outwards. The woman wore an ankle-length checked woollen skirt. A string, on which there were two amber beads, could be part of the metre-long cord bound up in her hair and which was also wound around her neck. Sewn in behind the outer cape were various small items, such as two thin leather thongs together with a horn comb and a narrow, colourful woven band, perhaps a hair band, wrapped in a piece of bladder. A scarf, it is presumed, ran over her shoulder and under her left arm where it was fastened with a bone pin.

The investigation report, written by district medical officer Steenberg, describes the inner cape as being fastened about the waist with a leather strap, which also secured the left arm. The right arm had been severed between the shoulder and the elbow and lay outstretched beside the body.

Later anatomical investigations revealed that the woman had an irregularly healed fracture to her left femur, so she would have walked with a limp. The severed right arm has been interpreted as the cause of death – she died of blood loss, according to one archaeologist. Even though the skin has today withdrawn from the fracture, it is unlikely ever to reveal whether the cut was administered at the time of, or before, her death – or even after, i.e. during subsequent peat cutting in the bog. A corresponding retraction of the skin can be seen on Tollund Man's left foot, which was first severed following examination in 1950 and later dried. The most recent investigations of Huldremose Woman have not been able to confirm the cause of her death, but the cord wound around her neck could suggest possible hanging or strangulation.

Huldremose Woman has been radiocarbon dated to around 130 BC.

AUNING GIRL, 1886

The body was found in the bog Dønmose near Gammel Estrup, to the east of Randers. Unfortunately it was already in a very poor state when it was recovered, because it was discovered by a peat cutter repeatedly treading on something hard. When he first caught sight of some skin he presumed, as in the case of Elling Woman, that he had found the remains of a drowned animal. A face then emerged from the bog so well-preserved that it 'had a clear expression of pain or as if crying', as the official from the museum in Randers described it in his report.

The head, hands and fingers and one breast of the deceased were well-preserved, whereas the remainder was badly damaged. A rectangular, woven piece of cloth, 153 x 101cm, as well as a very degraded but recognisable skin cape were found with the corpse.

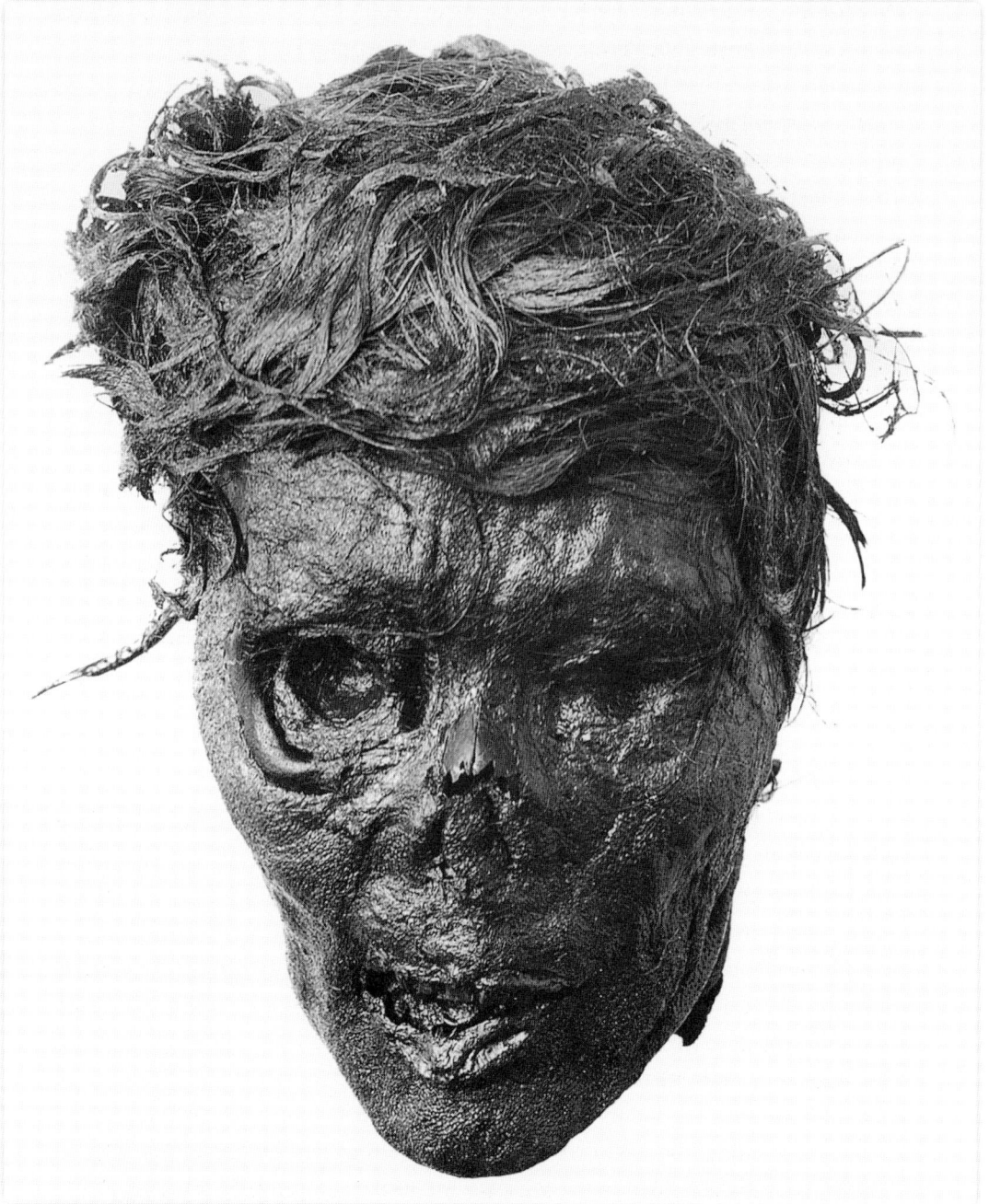

Roum Woman. The severed head after cleaning at the National Museum. *(Photo: The National Museum)*

At the time of its discovery the body was examined by district medical officer G. Hansen and general practitioner E. Hansen, who report that:

> Both arms were more or less well preserved with hands and fingers, on which there was even a single nail, but the skin and muscle tissue were in several places perforated so the bones protruded; large sections with internally intact flesh and fat, especially of one leg, were also very well preserved, and one breast which must have been quite plump was particularly clear and well preserved, and in addition to this of course a quantity of large and small parts of the skeleton; but clearest preserved was the head, on which the face had retained every furrow and every feature, even the finest.

But the doctors could not determine the cause of death.

An attempt was made to conserve the head using plaster of Paris but it ended up being stuffed with cotton wool, and it can be seen in this form today, exhibited at Museum Østjylland in Randers.

In 1981 a radiocarbon date was obtained for the body. One of the bones of the lower arm was used and the result revealed that Auning Girl died shortly before AD 1.

THE SEVERED HEAD FROM ROUM, 1942

The head, which was found during peat cutting in 1942, lay 1.5m below the bog surface, wrapped in a skin cape. It was very thoroughly investigated by the police in Hobro. An excerpt from the Police Register, police case no. 11/1942, gives an account of the investigation.

The chief constable and three detective constables met at farmer Jens Jonassen's peat bog on Roum Hede. District medical officer Andersen was summoned from Viborg and photographs were taken at the scene!

The district medical officer reports:

> A human head has been found which has been sewn into an animal skin with leather thongs. The head has been severed from the body at the level of the chin; the cut surface is rough so it can be concluded that a beheading has taken place. The soft tissues are relatively well preserved in that only the eyes and a little of the nose are missing. The eyebrows are fairly firmly attached; they are reddish in colour. The hair is darker, but more loosely attached; the individual hairs are 10–12cm long. The skin and soft tissues are soft, dough-like. The face is very delicate, oval, and the

teeth (the incisors) are well preserved, though black. One gets the impression that it is a woman.

To the relief of the police, the district medical officer was able to reveal that the head had been in the bog for a long time, perhaps hundreds of years.

The head was handed over to a representative of Hobro Museum, the architect Z. Zachariassen, who forwarded it to the National Museum. He asked for the head to be returned to Hobro Museum, following investigation, in order for it to be exhibited.

The response from the National Museum was the same as in the later case of Tollund Man – too macabre! The National Museum later transferred the head to the Normal-Anatomical Institute, where its dimensions were measured, after which it dried out. In 1976 it was found to be completely degraded.

The head has been radiocarbon dated to the time around AD 1.

THE BOG BODIES FROM SØGÅRDS MOSE NEAR SKIVE, 1942 AND 1944

These two discoveries were made only 200m apart. The body from 1942 is referred to as Daugbjerg Man, but often also as Søgård I Man, whereas that from 1944 is referred to as Søgård Man, though also as Søgård II Man.

Daugbjerg Man from 1942
At midsummer, labourer Jens Nielsen's spade struck a human skeleton, wrapped in a skin cape. A telephone message was sent to custodian Ramsdahl at Skive Museum, asking him to come as quickly as possible. The message arrived at 8.30 a.m. and he immediately began to cycle the 26km out to the bog, because 'peat production should be resumed as quickly as possible', as he wrote in his report. Fortunately he was picked up by a car on the way and he arrived at 10.30 a.m., but by that time too much had already happened: 'the entire find had been uncovered. The hair on the head had more or less gone; I found some tufts here and there and placed them by the neck.' At 11.30 a.m. the corpse was carried up onto dry land and next day it was sent in a crate to the National Museum as express goods. These were the prevailing circumstances for archaeological investigations of bog finds during the Second World War.

At the National Museum, textile expert Margrethe Hald wrote that:

Between the bog surface and the deceased lay a c. 2cm thick layer of cotton-grass. The corpse's head was bent backwards and the neck rested on the right lower arm. The right hand lay over the left shoulder, the hand was clenched, the fingers turned upwards and on two of them the nails were preserved. The left arm lay along the side with the heel of the hand by the pelvis. Both legs turned out to the left of the corpse, the knees were drawn up towards the chest and the heels towards the backside. In addition to the backbone, the shoulder blades and one hip socket were also visible. Hair-covered pieces of skin or hide covered the sides of the body and lay in under it. At the right side there was a skin cape which was almost completely preserved, whereas at the left side lay parts of one or two skin capes. On a level with the waist, by the left side of the body, lay a leather sandal, in which had been placed scraps of partially haired skin or hide as well as a tuft of horse hair. In under the body was the corresponding sandal, which contained a scrap of folded brown cloth. The sandals were joined together by the ends of the laces. There was, furthermore, a two-ply string of plant material at the waist.

The function of the string is unknown, but it demonstrates that plant fibres can be preserved in the acidic bog water. Consequently, clothes made of linen or nettle could, if present, also be preserved. The report relates that the corpse lay on a 2cm thick layer of cotton-grass. The sandals had been placed with the body and the largest of the capes had been laid alongside the body with the collar towards the feet.

There has been some doubt as to the sex of the corpse – Ramsdahl, who sent the body to the National Museum, writes: 'Hope you will take good care of the girl'. The medical examination carried out by K. Fischer-Møller states that the skull had shrunk significantly as a consequence of decalcification caused by acidity in the bog. The corpse's soft tissues had, for the most part, decomposed. Cartilage and ligaments were preserved. The body was probably that of a thirty to thirty-five year old individual with worn teeth.

In a letter to Skive Museum, the National Museum writes that the body was cleaned of soft tissues before it was sent to the Normal-Anatomical Institute, i.e. any possible remains of genitals would have been removed prior to the medical investigation.

The height is estimated at 170cm. The determination of sex, as already mentioned above, seems uncertain. However, at the time it was – erroneously – believed that skin capes were the exclusive preserve of men and the body therefore became male, but a degree of uncertainty persists.

The discovery of Daugbjerg Man in Søgårds Mose attracted great public interest. The spectators include the local village policeman who was summoned to the spot. *(Photo: Skive Museum)*

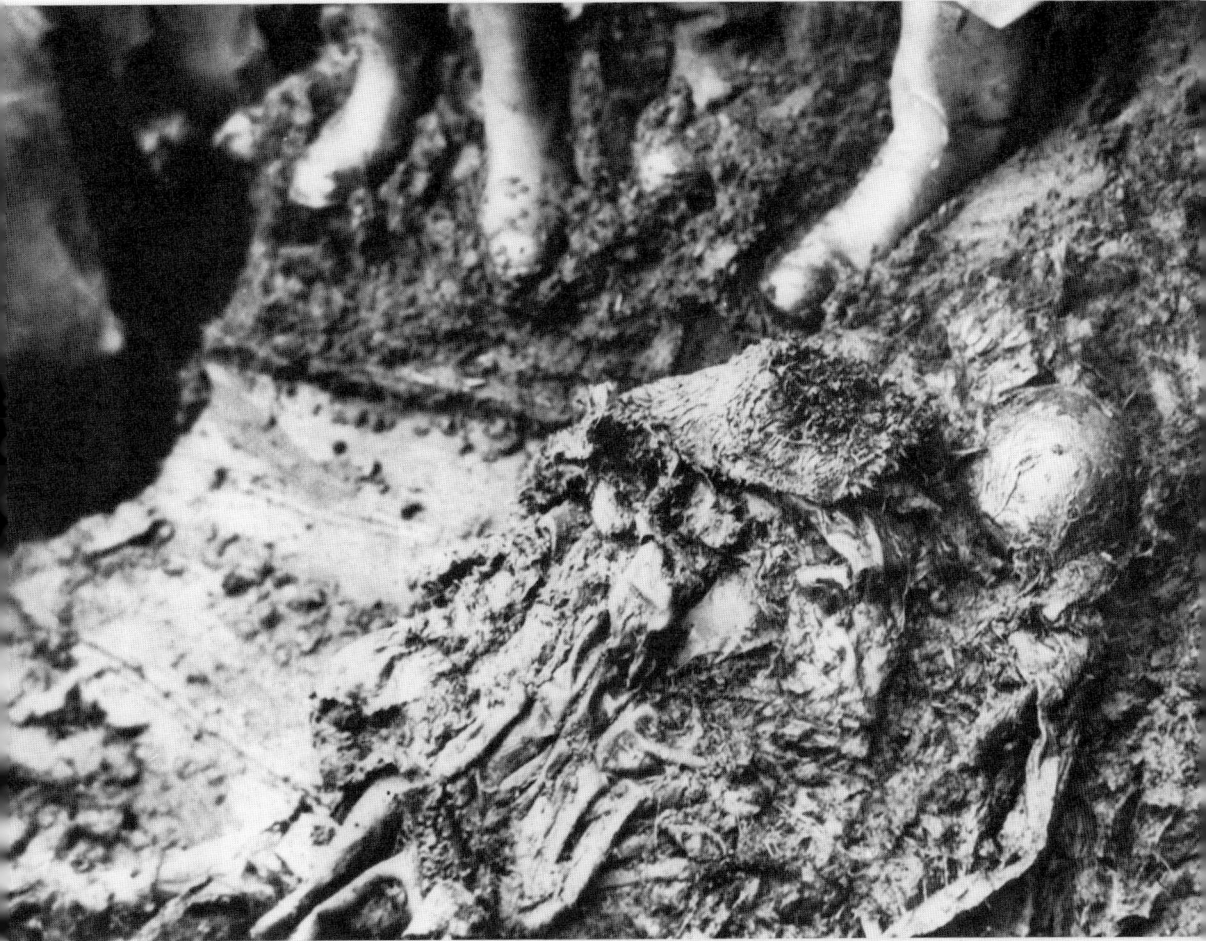

The discovery of Daugbjerg Man. The corpse can be seen lying within the peat. *(Photo: Skive Museum)*

In 1981 one of the capes was radiocarbon dated at the National Museum to 200 BC, and the body therefore dates from the Celtic Iron Age.

Søgård Man from 1944

In 1944 custodian Ramsdahl had again to make the 26km journey to Søgårds Mose; whether or not this was also by bicycle the report fails to mention. The new discovery lay 200m west of that from 1942.

The corpse lay at a depth of 2.2m, curled up and aligned in a north–south direction. It had been deposited in a cutting in the bog:

The labourer Valdemar Andreasen from Daugbjerg struck with his shovel the piece of
skin which lay over the feet of the corpse ... We managed to dig it free, then pushed
two long planks in under it, carried it thus until I sank in deep with one leg, with
great difficulty I managed to retrieve my leg ... The skeleton was very poorly preserved,
even the large bones and the skull were partially degraded, and were discarded on the
spot. Conversely, both hands and one foot were preserved, with flesh on.

In addition to the few skeletal parts, Ramsdahl reported that a cape was also found,
partially preserved, made of sheepskin, a tunic of calfskin, very well preserved,
together with two woven leggings.

   The woollen leggings are quite unique in a Danish context. The find demonstrates
clearly that the state of preservation of a bog body can vary greatly within a very
small area, even within a few centimetres. Hands and feet – the latter wrapped in
the leggings – were exceptionally well preserved, whereas the rest of the body was
either not preserved at all or in a very poor state. If the body had been recovered
without the presence of an expert it would be easy to conclude that only parts had
been deposited, and not an entire human corpse. The crate which the National
Museum received from Skive also contained part of the top of the skull with scalp
and hair intact. Conservator Knud Thorvildsen, who took delivery of the bog body
parts at the museum, relates that the well-preserved hands and feet were slowly
dried to bring them into the same state of 'preservation' (sic) as the National
Museum's other bog finds.

   It is possible that a medical investigation of the body took place, but it is unlikely
that any result was ever produced. Whether the body was of a man or a woman
is not known, but the presence of the cape, tunic and leggings has meant that it
has usually been considered as male. The cause of death, age and height are just
as uncertain. A radiocarbon analysis has been carried out on the skin cape which
indicates a date after the birth of Christ.

THE MAN FROM LYKKEGÅRDS MOSE NEAR RANDERS, 1945

In September 1945 the National Museum's archaeologist Povl Simonsen was
called to Lykkegårds Mose, where a human skeleton had been encountered. It
had already been taken up from the bog when Simonsen arrived, but all the parts,
apart from the lower left arm, were present. The body was that of a heavily-built
man in his twenties or thirties. The peat workers were unanimous that there was a
two-ply cord around his neck and, as mentioned in the report, this was confirmed

by La Cour, director of the company Nordisk Mosebrug, who had contacted the museum. The body had lain outstretched and facing upwards with the head to the west, at a depth of about 1m below the surface of the bog and 1.25m above its base.

The report ends by saying that a pollen sample was taken from one of the orbits of the skull and that the finder of the body received a reward of 15kr.

A later anatomical investigation revealed that the skull was dolichocephalic, typically Nordic and with a brain capacity of $1,670m^3$, and also that the height of the deceased had been 175cm. There were no fractures to the neck vertebrae – even so, he may well have been hanged (the cord around his neck), Tollund Man similarly shows no fractures of the neck vertebrae – and there were no bone abnormalities. The find is undated.

BORREMOSE MAN, 1946

The body of a man was found at a depth of 2m in an old cutting in the bog. The corpse appears to have been deposited in a sitting position in the bog.

The deceased had been hanged or strangled using a halter made of a three-ply bast rope which was still around his neck. On excavation, the back of his head was found to be crushed. This damage is today thought to be due to the pressure of the peat. The excavator believed that the attitude of the corpse corresponded to that in which it was deposited, but there was an important find of five detached toe nails around the knees. This shows the degree of disturbance that had taken place with respect to the body. This probably resulted from movements within the bog which are a consequence of the bog accumulating most rapidly in the centre. Gravity then forces the peat – like a glacier – to move slowly but powerfully outwards.

Some bog bodies, like Tollund Man, had largely avoided these movements. Whether they were located in the middle or on the outer margin of the raised bog could, in conjunction with other factors, have been crucial in determining whether bog bodies when discovered today give the impression of having been treated with care when deposited – or whether the dominant impression is of apparently having been subjected to torture, recognisable in the form of broken bones. The latter injuries could actually be due to the bog itself and not the people who deposited the body!

Borremose Man was naked but accompanied by two skin capes, both carefully made using the same sewing technique as Elling Woman's cape and Tollund Man's cap.

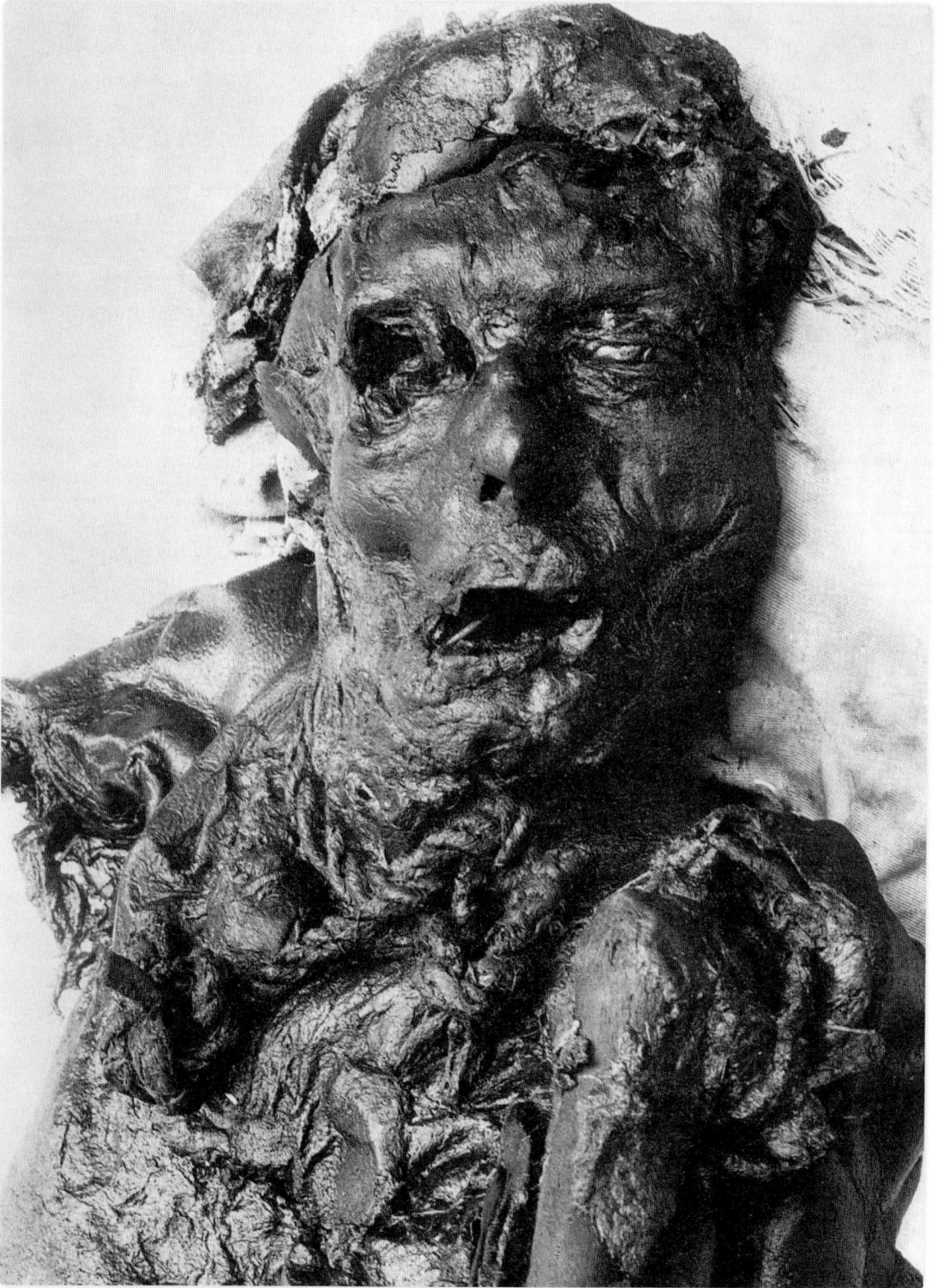

The bast rope demonstrates that the preservation of clothes, cord and rope made of vegetable fibres is possible in the acidic conditions of a raised bog. This is an important observation as it has often been maintained that the naked bog bodies could have worn clothes, but that these were made from vegetable fibres – nettle, flax and the like – and had therefore long ago decayed and disappeared without a trace. This example and others, including Daugbjerg Man, together with careful investigations of several well-preserved bodies, refute the assumption that bog bodies were not deposited naked but dressed in clothes of linen or nettle fibre which then disappeared in the acidic environment of the bog.

All three bog bodies from Borremose have been dated by the AMS method to the same time around 300 BC, i.e. the Celtic Iron Age.

BORREMOSE MAN, 1947

The body, which was that of a man, had been placed in an old peat cutting in the northern part of Borremose, about 1km from the previous year's find. Beneath and around the corpse were a number of branches with bark intact; however, it is unlikely that these had anything to do with the deposition of the body. The body was taken up from the bog in a block of peat on a zinc sheet and sent for further excavation at the National Museum. It was found about 2m beneath the surface of the bog.

After the body had been removed from the peat it was apparent that it had been placed on a thin layer of birch bark and that the peat around it was full of heather twigs. The corpse lay face-down in the peat cutting.

By the neck and chest of the body lay an amber bead, a circular 4mm thick bronze plate of 21–3mm in diameter and two pieces of leather thong bound together in a 'granny knot' around the neck. It is possible that the leather thong, the amber bead and the piece of bronze formed part of a necklace. Further to the thong at the neck there was another lying by the legs. This is not mentioned in the report but can be clearly seen on photographs and is briefly mentioned in a later article.

Opposite: Borremose Man 1946. He was hanged or strangled. *(Photo: The National Museum)*

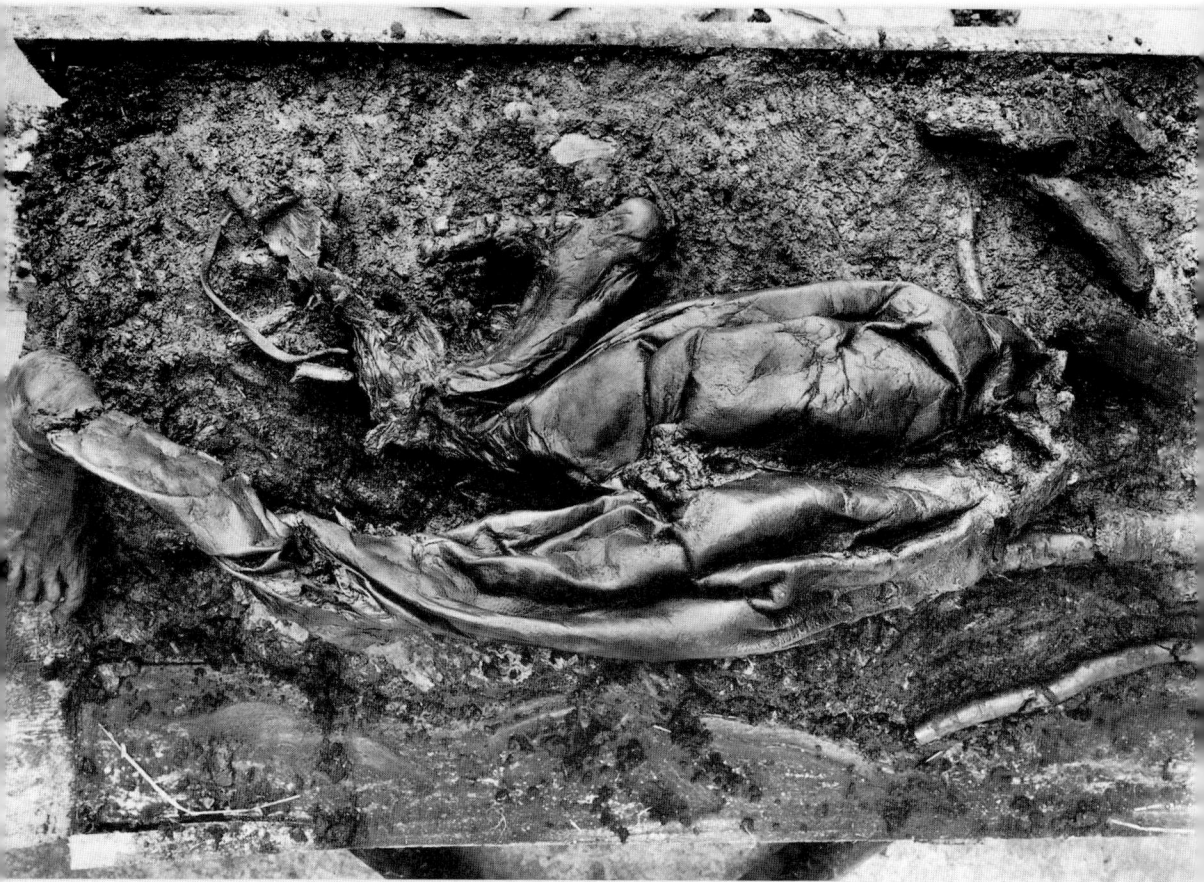

Borremose Man 1947. The position of his body on excavation showed that the 'natural movements' of the raised bog could move the bog bodies around and often inflict severe damage. *(Photo: The National Museum)*

Could the leather thong around the neck together with that found by the corpse's legs have been the cause of death? The ends of both thongs had been cut off squarely and they are of the same thickness.

It is unusual to find ornaments with a bog body, but just as unusual was the fact that a pot lay by the left leg of the body, together with two bones from a child. The ornaments are probably the reason that the body was initially referred to as that of a woman. The excavator, Elise Thorvildsen, writes in her report that the genitals were poorly preserved but she was, however, able to identify the body as being male.

Two woollen blankets and a woollen shawl were found wrapped around the legs of the corpse. The pottery vessel is consistent with a date in the Celtic Iron Age.

BORREMOSE WOMAN, 1948

In 1948 the bog yielded up a third bog body within as many years. As in the case of the others, the body was taken up lying within a block of peat and sent to the National Museum for further excavation and examination.

This time the corpse was found to be that of a woman who, like the others, had been deposited in an old peat cutting. An examination of the bog stratigraphy revealed that the surface of the body was covered by matted roots. In a lecture to the British Society in London in 1972 the excavator, Børge Brorson Christensen, reported that the material was cotton-grass. The find site was believed to have been too wet for the plant to be able to grow there. Consequently, the cotton-grass must have been picked with the particular intention of placing it around the body.

The corpse lay face down in the bog. It was of very modest height, only 143cm, but some shrinkage had almost certainly occurred as seen in the case of other bog bodies. The woman was unusually plump. The excavation report states with respect to her backside that: 'This part of the body had been exceptionally well developed.' The genitalia were intact and left no doubt as to her sex.

The corpse was wrapped in a woollen blanket measuring 175 x 115cm. A series of holes, a leather cord and some folds make it seem likely that the blanket constituted a kind of skirt.

The immediate cause of death appears to have been a heavy blow to the head inflicted from the front. This had almost completely crushed the lower part of the face, the chin and the cheeks. The scalp, with intact hair, had been torn off and lay mostly over, or in continuation of, the remains of the head. A large piece of the scalp – with hair – lay against the neck and the right hand.

The hands and feet were rather well preserved but, as in the case of the body from 1946, almost all the nails had become detached. Six of them were, however, found in the vicinity of their original position. They demonstrate that the body must have moved after being placed in the bog – one of the nails even lay under the covering cloth.

Seen in conjunction with the fact that the scalp with intact hair had also been spread about, this suggests that the pressure and movements of the bog had changed the attitude of the body. The pressure can also explain the severe damage now apparent to the woman's head. New pathological investigations have also sown well-justified doubt with respect to the violent extent of the cause of death.

Borremose Woman 1948, plump and displaying severe injuries, particularly to the back of the head. The injuries were caused by the pressure of the bog. *(Photo: The National Museum)*

GRAUBALLE MAN, 1952

Grauballe Man was discovered in the bog Nebelgaard Mose in 1952. The bog is located immediately north-east of Silkeborg, but news of the find went from the peat cutters via doctor Ulrik Balslev in Aidt to Professor P.V. Glob, who investigated the discovery on-site and subsequently took the body back to the Aarhus Museum. In doing so, he ensured the corpse was well taken care of and that it came to be perceived as a significant prehistoric discovery which, with virtually no scruples, could be presented to the public, even though the man was stark naked. However, the museum's conservator did 'smooth out' Grauballe Man's heavily distorted face so it appeared more 'human'. This was a major mistake judged by modern professional norms, but in 1952 it was seen as being necessary – otherwise it would be much too macabre a sight!

Grauballe Man was about thirty years of age, or slightly older when he died. He was killed by having his throat slit from ear to ear. Later medical examinations raised the possibility that a competing cause of death could be a fractured skull, at the upper right side of the head and temple region, caused by a blow. Grauballe Man's left tibia was also broken, something which could have happened either before or after death. At the time of his discovery, the blows to his forehead and his shin were explained by the fact that his throat could not have been cut without first having knocked him unconscious and possibly also broken his leg in order to prevent him from running away.

New medical investigations carried out in connection with a timely overhaul and cleaning of the body revealed that the fractures need not necessarily have been

Nebelgårds Mose, a small kettlehole bog which, until 1952, contained the body of Grauballe Man. The bog lies just north of Silkeborg. *(Photo: Silkeborg Museum)*

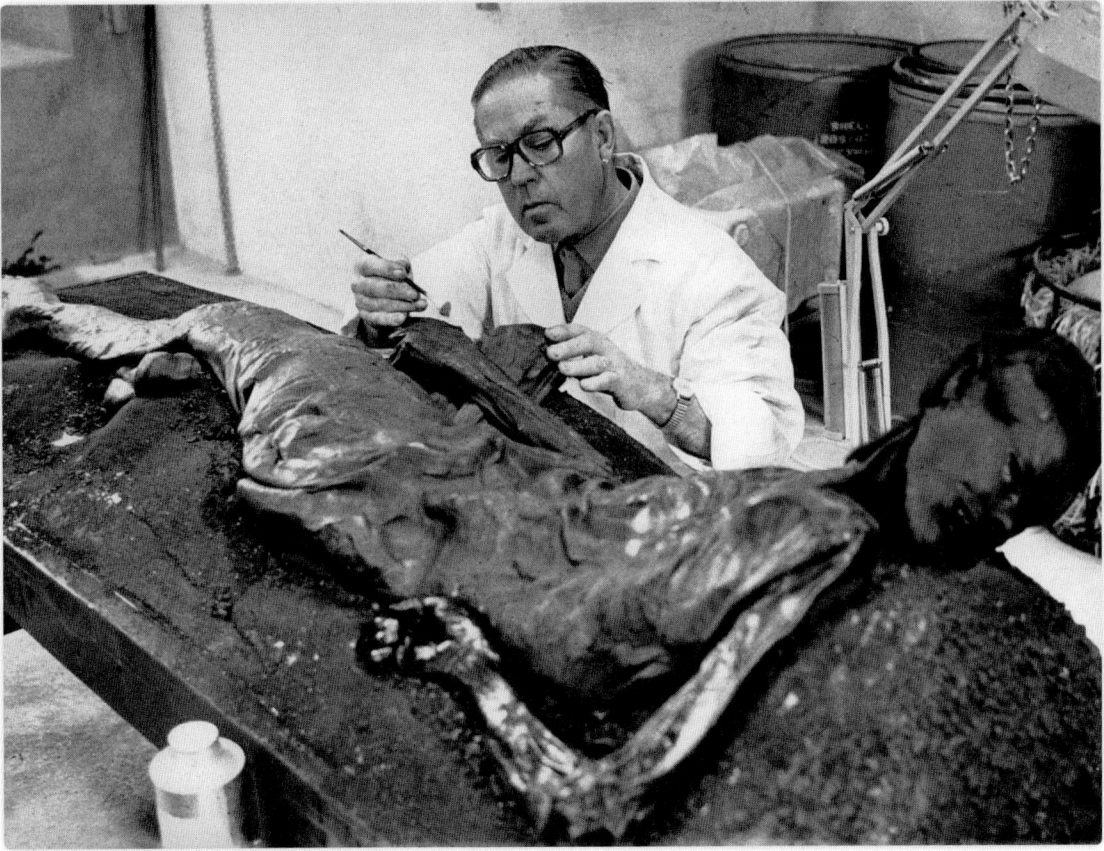

Grauballe Man in the block of peat immediately after excavation. Conservation with tannic acid. *(Photo: P.V. Glob)*

inflicted before or in connection with the cutting of his throat – they probably all occurred as a consequence of pressure exerted by the surrounding peat in the bog.

The fractures evident on Grauballe Man's corpse have been used in support of a theory that the people who later became bog bodies were subjected to extreme violence when they met their deaths, far exceeding that which was the actual cause of death – so-called 'overkill'. They were criminals on whom one vented one's fury!

Similar instances of 'overkill' were said to apply to the Borrremose bodies and the woman from Huldremose. As in the case of Grauballe Man, new medical investigations have shown that these fractures very probably took place post mortem – a consequence of pressure within the bog.

Grauballe Man was placed in the bog completely naked and no objects, such as clothing, pots or tools, were recorded in the vicinity. This is very much an exception with respect to well-preserved bog bodies. It is theoretically possible that peat cutting in former times has removed such items, but this seems unlikely.

Grauballe Man was initially radiocarbon dated to AD 310; a date which subsequently proved to be out by more than 600 years – he is from around 290 BC, the Celtic Iron Age, like Tollund Man and the other bog bodies.

The fact that a nearby bog has at some point in time also been the scene of disturbing discoveries or incidents is suggested by its name Djævlemosen (Devil's Bog) and the farm to which the bog belongs is known, similarly unusually, as Djævlemosegård (Devil's Bog Farm)!

LINDOW MOSS, 1983 – THE MURDER IN THE BOG

The find circumstances for Lindow Man and the investigations which followed were very special and fully lived up to the drama that has surrounded several other bog body discoveries.

As with Tollund Man, it started as a criminal investigation. Whilst the case of Tollund Man was quickly resolved as being a matter for archaeologists, the discovery of Lindow Man gave rise to an actual modern criminal case.

It was on 13 May 1983 while two peat workers, Andy Mould and Stephen Dooley, were keeping an eye on the conveyor belt on the edge of the peat bog which took the peat up from the bottom of the bog to a tipping wagon. Their job was to remove foreign objects from the peat, especially branches, before it was finely broken up and spread out to dry. A round object appeared on the conveyor belt, about 20cm in diameter. They removed it, noting that it was soft and, in fun, called it a dinosaur egg. The foreman thought it was a punctured football and told them to throw it away. But the men's curiosity was awakened and they then realised it was a human head. The police were called.

A pathologist carried out a detailed investigation and concluded that the head was of a woman of European appearance, of about thirty to fifty years of age. The discovery was probably the crucial clue in an open murder case!

At the time of the discovery, the police in Macclesfield, a town close to Lindow Moss, were in the process of interviewing two people suspected of a number of crimes. What perhaps interested the police most of all was that the suspects were able to reveal that a former cell mate, Peter Reyn-Bardt, had told them that about twenty years previously he had murdered his wife, Malika. He had dismembered

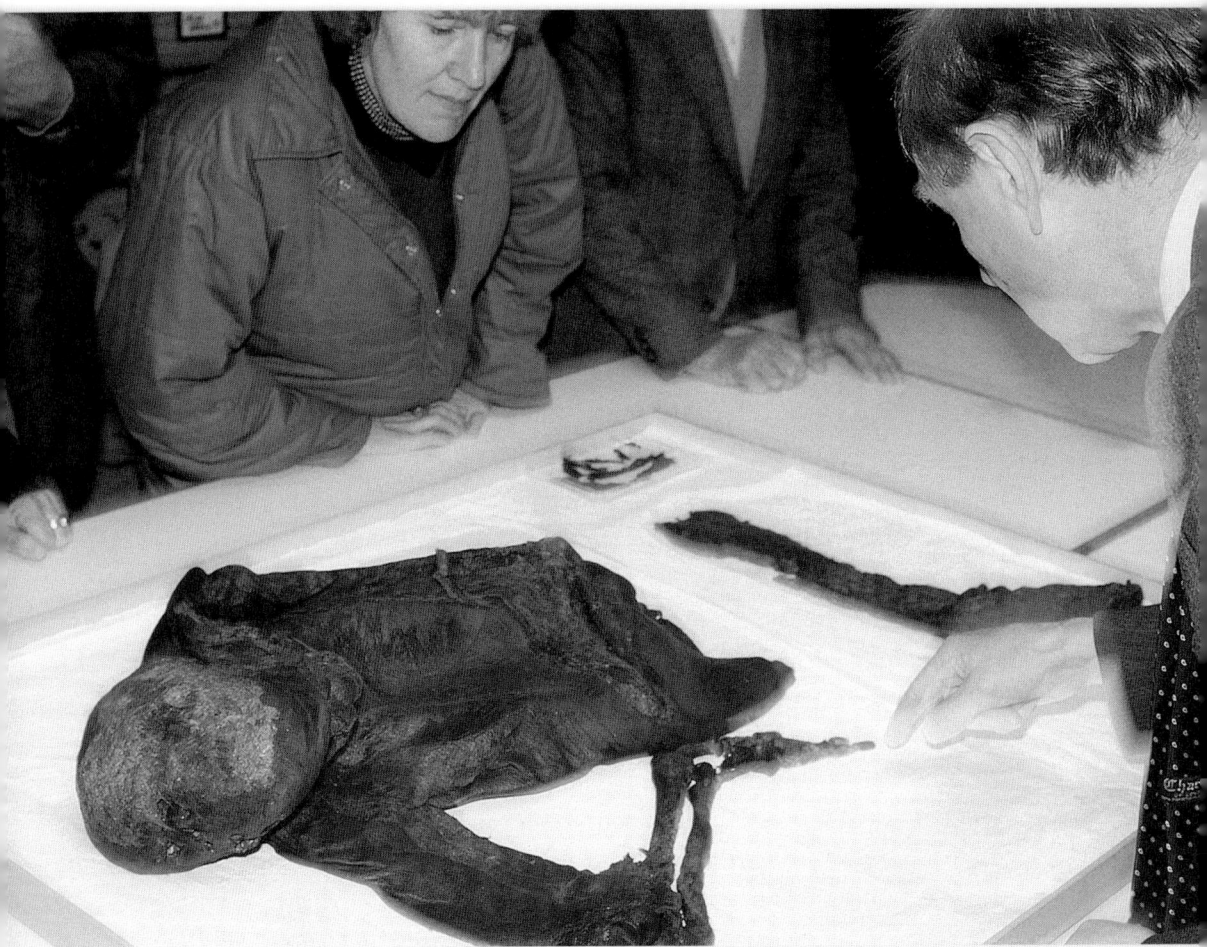

Lindow Man at the British Museum. Silkeborg Museum was invited inside for a closer look. The body is being presented by Dr I.M. Stead. *(Photo: Silkeborg Museum)*

the body, burnt it and buried it in his garden which, very unfortunately for him, bordered on Lindow Moss.

The police had previously excavated Reyn-Bardt's garden with no result and without a body they had, of course, no case. But now his wife's head had apparently turned up 300m from the house. On hearing this, and without the police informing him of the precise distance, Reyn-Bardt made a full confession. In court he was convicted of murder on his own confession. It is very unusual in British criminal history for someone to be convicted of murder without having the body of the victim as evidence. One can speculate whether Reyn-Bardt would have confessed had he known that the head which was found would subsequently be revealed by radiocarbon dating to be 1,740 years old. His long prison sentence has since given him time to think about it.

On 1 August another foreign object appeared on the conveyor belt. This time it was a human foot and it led to the discovery of the remainder of the corpse. However, the police were not minded to turn the matter over to archaeologists because they still 'lacked' Malika Reyn-Bardt's body.

The police were only convinced that this was also an archaeological find after the British Museum proved, via an express radiocarbon analysis, that it was a museum matter, put in place a series of conservation initiatives and successfully argued that these new body parts probably belonged to the head which had been found previously.

Subsequently the remains of one or two further corpses were located. The uncertainty with respect to the number is because the parts were found scattered and could represent one or two individuals. So far it has not proved possible to extract intact DNA from bog bodies, otherwise we would be able to resolve the matter conclusively. The body parts are from prehistory and Malika's body remains to be found!

WINDEBY GIRL – THE 'POLITICAL' BOG BODY

Domlandsmoor in Southern Schleswig is part of Windeby Manor. The bog body found here in 1952 is the one which has provided greatest support for interpretations maintaining that bog bodies were society's outcasts – homosexuals, cowards/deserters and adulterers – whereas less dramatic explanations have been pushed into the background.

Following excavation, conservation and exhibition, this rather well-preserved bog body proved to be that of a young woman with a shaved head (some say scalped!), blind-folded with a hair band and making a finger gesture suggesting that she had broken with the strict sexual moral code of the time.

That same year another bog body was found in the vicinity. This was of a man who had been strangled, secured to the bottom of the peat cutting with eight sticks, and suddenly the story began to make sense: this was her lover! And the story could, furthermore, be 'confirmed' by a Classical source on the history of the Germans, written in AD 98 by the Roman author Tacitus (AD 56–120), and later by the Irish monk St Boniface (c. AD 675–754).

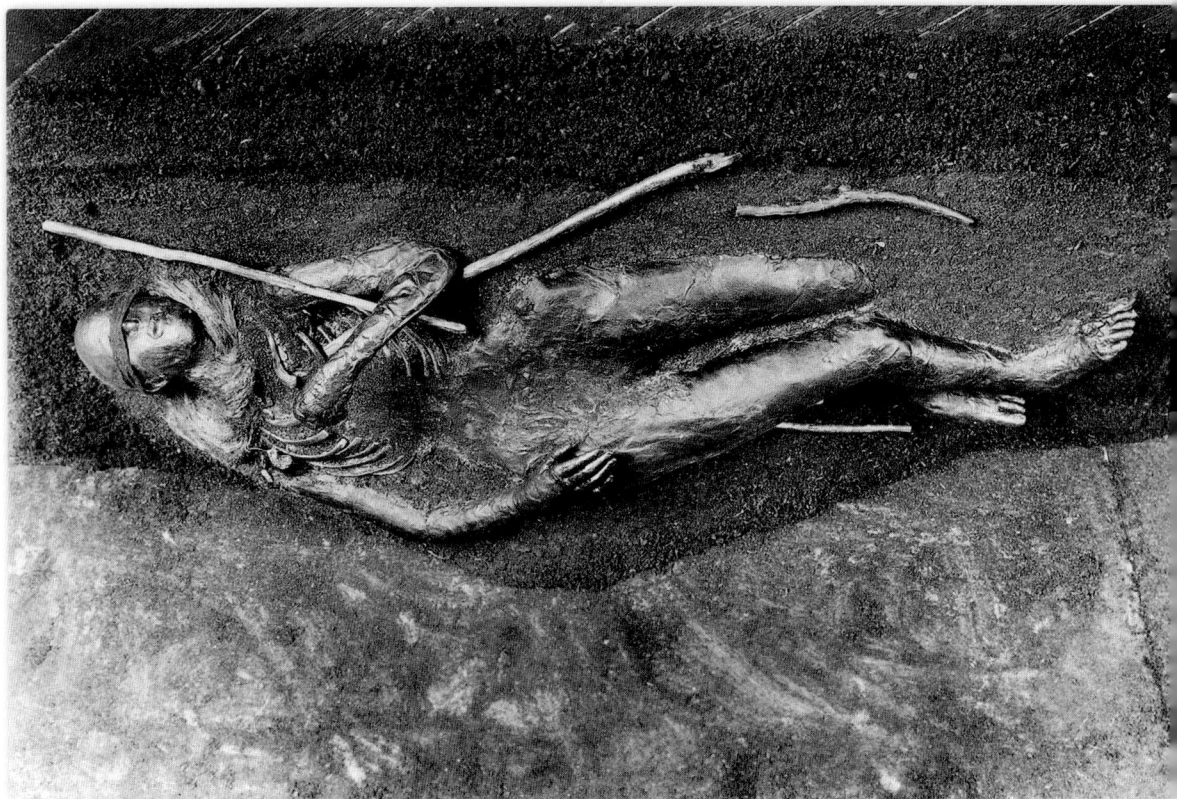

Windeby Girl as exhibited at Schloss Gottorf. *(Photo: Landesmuseum Schloss Gottorf)*

This dramatic interpretation has been explained in recent years as being in accordance with an ideology employed by notorious archaeologists in SS uniforms in an attempt to find evidence in support of the Germans' historical right to supremacy. German archaeology's influential professor Herbert Jankuhn, who interpreted the fate of the German bog bodies, was one of the leading SS archaeologists/soldiers until the very end of the war.

Subsequently, more detailed studies of the find in situ in the bog have revealed that the hair band, which in the exhibition today is placed over the girl's eyes, was placed there by a conservator. On excavation it lay across the middle of her face, not over her eyes. The 'provocative' finger gesture is also a product of the conservator's imagination. In the exhibition it can be seen that the thumb of the girl's right hand is placed between the index and the middle finger – this displays a so-called mano fico gesture. In the Greek-Roman world this was perceived as an obscene gesture on a par with the way in which an extended middle finger is regarded today.

On excavation the thumb was actually between the ring and the middle finger – and this cannot be identified with anything obscene!

The girl's hair had been cut very short and uneven in two stages – the right side first, then the left. Neither is it correct that she was naked: about her neck was the collar of a skin cape; the remainder of the cape and the parts of her body beneath it were not preserved.

On the basis of her build – plump thighs, but graceful bones – it was assumed that she came from a wealthy family who, by virtue of her death, had probably re-established their 'honour'. The plump thighs are, however, a product of the conservator's perception of the situation and cannot be confirmed from the actual observations.

New impartial investigations clearly show that this is the body of a young girl or, more probably, a boy, of about fourteen years of age, who periodically suffered illness or malnutrition as revealed by the presence of 'Harris lines' in their bone structure. The corpse was also surrounded by four pottery vessels. The body found nearby, the 'lover', was not secured with sticks; instead, branches lay over the 'man' whose sex has actually not been determined. In the case of both the child and the adult, the genitalia were not preserved.

Radiocarbon analyses reveal a date for the death for Windeby Girl immediately after AD 1, whereas the nearby 'man' is from the period 385–185 BC. The most likely reading of the situation is as follows: This Windeby Girl is a girl or boy of thirteen-fourteen years of age, who at times suffered hunger, wearing a normal hairstyle (on the left side of the head the hair is a little shorter than that of Tollund Man) and with normal clothing (skin cape). The pots placed with the body contained food and drink for the journey to the Kingdom of the Dead – as in a normal Iron Age burial, but carried out in a wetland area. Windeby Girl's circumstances conform to normal Iron Age burial practice.

Similar burials have now also been found in Denmark. The well-preserved Lønne Hede grave, dating from the same period as Windeby Girl, was also situated in a wetland area, and this also resulted in the preservation of her clothes and coiffure.

With respect to the 'lover', 'he' is probably a 'normal' bog body from the Celtic Iron Age, throttled or strangled with a halter of hazel. Quite by coincidence, 'his' fate was to be deposited in a place in the bog where a normal burial would take place several centuries later.

COMMON CHARACTERISTICS OF DANISH BOG BODIES FROM THE CELTIC IRON AGE

The ability of bogs to preserve animal material is amply illustrated by the bog bodies themselves. But plant material can also be well preserved – sticks, wooden peat spades, ladders and the cotton-grass upon which several bog bodies rested are all in exceptionally good condition. In the case of the bog body from Daugbjerg, a rope made of vegetable fibres was found at the waist. There is therefore no evidence to assume anything other than that Tollund Man was naked when deposited in the bog, apart from his cap and the belt around his waist.

Elling Woman was similarly naked beneath her cape, apart from her woven belt. It has been debated whether her belt was outside the cape, holding it close to the body, or whether it sat about her hips beneath the cape, and she was naked beneath it. The evidence tends to suggest the latter was the case as there are no openings in the cape for the arms and it has no folds suggesting it has been laced together. If the belt had sat outside the cape, the arms would have been bound idly beneath it.

'The bog body family'. (Drawing: Flemming Bau)

Several of the bog bodies although naked (apart from a belt), have clothes next to or over them. It is possible that Tollund Man may originally have been clothed, but that his clothing was woven of vegetable fibres such as flax (linen) which perhaps could not survive the time spent in the bog.

Such speculations were entered into by Knud Thorvildsen when, at very close quarters, he dealt with the bog body found in 1946 in Borremose:

> The corpse was completely naked, as bog bodies often are. It has, from time to time, been maintained that this nakedness was not the original state, but was due to the bodies having been clad in thin linen which in the course of time has perished, in contrast to woollen clothes which, if they have accompanied the deceased, are almost always exceptionally well preserved. In this particular case there is unlikely to have been a costume of linen which has now vanished. The conditions for preservation are so good that even the finest piece of clothing would have left its mark, if in no other way then as an impression in the peat which lay immediately against the skin; but not the least observation was made in this direction despite the fact that attention was turned towards this possibility.

The numbers of male and female bog bodies are more or less equal. It is, however, striking that there are no examples from Denmark (in contrast to Germany and The Netherlands) of children laid in bogs, sacrificed and placed in such a way that they became bog bodies.

In the case of the bog bodies from Krogens Møllemose and Borremose 1947 there are also indications that they could have been hanged.

8

FROM DARK PATCHES OF SOIL TO A SOCIETY

Archaeologists, equipped only with teaspoons, excavating frantically in a race against huge construction machines. This stereotyped perception of archaeology and the threat to our heritage was at times harsh reality until the mid-1960s; then archaeologists took control of the earth-moving machines. The few dark patches that had previously appeared in the subsoil after days of hard work removing a small area of topsoil with a shovel and carting away the spoil with a wheelbarrow now began to form coherent patterns. And where large areas of subsoil could be exposed by machine, the remains were suddenly revealed of past houses, fences, graves and defensive works.

The difference made by the use of mechanical excavators can be briefly illustrated as follows: before machines were employed, Silkeborg Museum had not excavated the remains of a single prehistoric house, even though the topsoil at the museum's excavation sites contained potsherds, quern stones and burnt daub. The latter clearly illustrate the presence of an Iron Age village. Since hydraulic excavators, JCB diggers and bulldozers made their entrée, traces have been discovered of more than 1,000 houses dating from the Neolithic, Bronze Age and Iron Age. And examples dating from the Viking Age and the Middle Ages have now also been added to the list.

Not only do we now find traces of individual houses, we can also uncover the physical environment encompassing these small societies. Traces of everyday enterprises appear as large dark patches in the subsoil – where clay was dug to make daub for walls, as a floor covering and for the production of pots. Refuse from daily activities provides an excellent insight into everyday life and we often have the good fortune to find it because it has been discarded in these very empty clay pits these dark patches suddenly reflect a society!

FARMSTEADS AND VILLAGES

Traces of the actual houses are, as a rule, not visible at the surface, but their presence is apparent to the sharp-eyed archaeologist who notices potsherds, burnt flint, quern stones, hammer stones and iron slag. If a metal detector survey has also turned up ornaments and other prehistoric metal objects, it's a clear-cut case. A mechanical excavator is brought onto the scene to remove the disturbed plough soil and expose the underlying, almost untouched, subsoil of sand, clay and gravel. In the past, when a prehistoric builder needed to erect a post for the

Mechanical excavators have largely replaced the small hand tools for which archaeologists are renowned. The machine has just uncovered an Iron Age pot. The next layer removed by the machine revealed the remains of an Iron Age house, evident as dark patches in the subsoil. *(Photo: Silkeborg Museum)*

vertical construction of a house or stalls for animals, he had to dig a hole which cut deep down into the pale subsoil. He – and it could well have been Tollund Man – stood the post in the hole and secured it by back-filling with the material he had just dug out and stamping it firmly into place. Sometimes a small pot containing a little food would be placed beside the post – a gift to the gods or the spirits who had perhaps been disturbed by the building activities!

As these prehistoric houses were very combustible, thunderstorms were greatly feared and so an iron knife might also be added to the construction with its tip pointing upwards, to catch the lightning. A flint axe, thousands of years older than the house, could perform the same preventative function.

A knife was found in the large outbuilding of a settlement at Gjern dating from Tollund Man's time. The long blade had been placed alongside one of the building's roof-bearing posts, the tip pointing upwards. The fact that this was not always enough to ward off this very danger was abundantly clear from the thick burnt layer which lay over the knife. The farm had been destroyed by a fierce fire; perhaps it was struck by lightning after all.

A few decades after a house had been built it was gone again – moved, burnt or simply collapsed and decayed so nothing visible remained at the surface. But in the subsoil the holes from the posts were still apparent as dark patches. The posts had rotted and given up their colouring – charcoal resulting from a charring process to which the lower part had been subjected to slow down decay. The earth which the Iron Age man had stamped down around the posts as he built now also had a different colour from that of the subsoil. It had become mixed with the dark topsoil, leading archaeologists on the trail.

The actual floors of the houses, where life unfolded both in the living area and the byre, usually lies scattered and fragmented in the soil above and around the house site – ploughed to pieces long ago. These remains can provide important information with respect to the age of the house but in our mechanical age there is rarely the opportunity for detailed examination of the soil before modern roads or buildings cover the spot. Fortunately, large numbers of potsherds are usually associated with an Iron Age house and these can reveal its age. The old joke about archaeologists and their obsession with potsherds is true insofar as these sherds – unremarkable as they often appear – are of crucial importance for the dating of Iron Age settlements. The shape and ornamentation of these pots changes through time. In most of Denmark people in the Iron Age lived in one spot for a couple of generations then moved on to a new site close by. There could be practical reasons for this: the old village had become run-down and its area, well-manured by the daily presence of humans and animals, was better served by being

Dark patches in the subsoil trace the outline of a typical rectangular Iron Age house. *(Photo: Silkeborg Museum)*

cultivated. Moreover, the difficulties in reconstructing the buildings elsewhere were no greater than renovating the existing ones where they stood. Other factors, such as fluctuations in climate, could also have played a role. In wet periods there would have been a preference for higher, drier ground, and in drier periods it would have been better to live closer to the damp meadowlands.

Common to all Iron Age periods is that the houses were rectangular and lay oriented east–west. Their length could vary from 15 to 20m and their width from 5 to 8m. In the middle of each of the two side walls there was a door with a threshold which led into a small room located between the living quarters at one end and the byre at the other. Between these doors there would almost always have been a draught and it was here people would thresh the grain. After threshing, the chaff could, with the aid of the wind, be separated from the grain – winnowed – by throwing the mixture into the air. The heavy grain fell to the floor; the lighter chaff was blown away – possibly explaining the origin of the word 'threshold': it kept the crop within the house when 'threshing'.

In the west end of the house, the family lived on low benches set around the open fire. In the east end was a byre fitted out with stall dividers. The vicinity of humans and animals would have provided warmth to supplement that from wood or peat burnt on the hearth. Sensitive archaeologists have expressed the view that people lived in the west end so the prevailing western wind would keep the smell of the byre away from the living quarters. Others, of a more practical persuasion, hold the contrary view that the eastern wind, which blows when it is coldest, led warmth from the byre into the living quarters. The latter explanation may well have some truth about it. It seems unlikely that people would have been bothered by the smell of the animals – the close proximity must have led to everyone and everything – humans and animals – smelling more or less the same. Flies, on the other hand, would have been a terrible plague and the numbers of mice must also have quite been a problem. It was not until later in the Iron Age, in the first centuries AD, that those inveterate mouse hunters – the domestic cat and the stone marten – apparently arrived in Denmark. The dog, however, had faithfully followed at the heel of humans since the Mesolithic.

The houses were three aisled, with the roof being carried by two parallel rows of internal free-standing posts. The walls were of wattle and daub and the roof was thatched with straw, heather twigs, heather turf or grass turves. There were also some houses without byres and also smaller buildings, but most of the buildings were long-houses – the standard house of the bog body period.

The phenomenon of villages moving a short distance every few generations – so-called 'wandering villages' – continued, with a few regional exceptions, until the introduction of Christianity in the Viking Age. In this respect the church and churchyard, which were fixed, together with changes in agrarian practices could have had a crucial influence. A picture seems to emerge of Iron Age villages having been located around our present-day villages, and they could very well have been their predecessors.

Whereas only the outlines of houses from his time are visible in Tollund Man's area, there were quite different building traditions in Northern Jutland. People here stayed in the same place and built new houses on top of the remains of the old worn-out ones. House followed house until an actual mound, a 'tell', was formed, resulting in thick protective layers. These have provided archaeologists with good opportunities to take a closer look and gain an impression of the life that unfolded there.

Settlements from Tollund Man's time – the Celtic Iron Age – have been discovered and excavated in Central Jutland, but to date none have been close enough to be possible candidates for 'his' settlement, or that of Elling Woman. One settlement, excavated near the river Gjern Å, north-east of Bjældskovdal, had eight long-houses. These lay scattered and were not particularly large: 10m long and 4.5–5m wide. All had living quarters in the west end and a byre to the east, the latter with room for six cows. This was not a large herd, but when supplemented by crop cultivation, gathering wild plant foods and hunting it would have been enough to support a family.

THE VILLAGE POTTER

At a short distance from the houses, archaeologists found pits where clay had been dug. This was primarily for building construction, but probably also for making pots – there was a potter in the village. The actual place where the pots were coiled, smoothed and burnished was not discovered but the pottery kilns, which for reasons of fire-safety were located a good distance from the houses, did turn up. The ground plans of these roughly 4m long kilns were almost figure-of-eight shaped; one half was the actual kiln itself whereas the other, located in front of the stoking hole, functioned as an ash pit.

To the good fortune of archaeologists and probably to the great dismay of the village potter, the best-preserved kiln had collapsed during the last firing. Beneath the collapsed dome lay at least 65kg of potsherds from which the museum's conservator was able to re-assemble various types of pottery vessel – in total about fifty whole vessels out of the estimated sixty present.

The excavation was hindered by snow and frost – conditions that must be faced by archaeologists when a developer is waiting to get digging. Perhaps the most important result of the investigation was that yet another settlement from the same time lay within view, only a few hundred metres away; this had three or four farmsteads. The two settlements could look over at one another and, if the wind was in the right direction, they could smell the smoke from each other's fires and hear the calling of their animals. On the meadowlands along the river Gjern Å, the herdsmen and shepherds must have had difficulty keeping their animals apart when they went home in the evenings.

At a safe distance from an Iron Age village located by the river Gjern Å lay the remains of a collapsed potter's kiln. It contained the last firing comprising about sixty pottery vessels. The kiln's collapse was a disaster for the potter but a piece of luck for the archaeologists. *(Photo: Silkeborg Museum)*

LARGE AND SMALL IN ONE VILLAGE

The village of Hodde in Western Jutland, which was excavated in full in the 1980s, had its origins at the end of the Celtic Iron Age and functioned over the course of five to six generations. In addition to the numerous house remains representing several consecutive building phases, there were also traces of the fences that had enclosed the individual farmsteads. The fenced area, and the size of the houses within the fences, revealed the existence of four economic and social layers in the village.

To date, however, Hodde remains unique with respect to its size and degree of detail, and the question remains whether Tollund Man lived in a village like Hodde or in a smaller village such as that seen at Gjern. Excavations in Tollund Man's local area tend to suggest the latter.

Returning to Hodde, the wealthiest people in the village lived in a farm, the chieftain's or magnate's farm, with a built area of 200m². The farm had one of the village's largest long-houses, augmented by two smaller buildings. In the farm's first phase the long-house had room for about thirty animals in its byre.

The next social layer had farms with a built area of 110–130m², comprising a long-house and two smaller buildings. The long-house had room for sixteen to twenty-two animals. There were between one and four farms of this type.

Most of the farms belonged to the third socio-economic layer; these had a built area of 50–100m². The majority consisted of a single house with room for fourteen to sixteen animals; some did, however, have a further one to two buildings associated with them.

Farms from the lowest layer in village society consisted of a single long-house with a built area of 45–50m² and apparently had no byre.

FIELDS AND CROPS

The fields of the various villages must have bordered each other – these were no small isolated settlements but a society where it was easy to come into contact with one another. The neighbouring village lay no further away than it was possible to smell the smoke from its fires. Fortification of the villages has been demonstrated but this appears to have been far from common. The villages and the individual farms were often fenced but the fences probably served to keep the animals in at night and out during the day, rather than as protection against hostile attacks.

The remains of a burnt building have provided excellent information relative to an understanding of the last meals eaten by Tollund Man, Grauballe Man and Borremose Man. Towards the end of the Celtic Iron Age a fire destroyed a farm with a subterranean granary – a gain cellar – at Overbygård in Southern Vendsyssel.

The fire came suddenly and nothing could be saved from the well-stocked store. It contained more than sixty pots and almost a quarter of them were completely undamaged; in addition there were wooden vessels and baskets.

The greatest asset to archaeologists was, however, that the pots contained more than 100 litres of charred grain and seeds. This is the largest find of its kind from Danish prehistory.

It provides a unique opportunity to see what Iron Age people stored in their granaries and it seems the composition corresponds closely to the food that Tollund Man and the other bog bodies had eaten.

In the Celtic Iron Age, naked barley was the most common cereal type but bread wheat was also abundant, accompanied by emmer, oats, hulled barley, flax and gold of pleasure. In at least one of the heaps of grain at Overbygård, naked barley and wheat were found mixed together. However, it is very unlikely they were grown together; they were probably mixed after threshing and processing. Several of the pots were found to contain large quantities of weed seeds.

The snapshot picture from the Overbygård granary confirms that the mixture of grain and weed seeds found in the guts of Tollund Man, Borremose Man and Grauballe Man was not something that was especially selected for the occasion. The food which they had eaten shortly before they died could have been obtained from an ordinary store or granary. There is no indication that there was a special 'cultic' meal.

Arable fields such as those which provided Tollund Man with his food have been known archaeologically for a long time. However, they were not always recognised as such – being termed 'churchyards' or 'defensive works' – because the structures discovered consisted of stone dykes enclosing rectangular areas.

No prehistoric fields are found in places where the soil has been cultivated in modern times – any trace of them has been completely erased by ploughing. But in areas of forest and where 're-cultivation' has not taken place, Iron Age field systems are well preserved. Prior to the advent of modern agriculture and forestry, Iron Age field systems covered such large areas that the authorities abandoned in advance any form of formal protection – scheduling – which would otherwise apply to other categories of ancient monuments.

In the period 1878–81, Chamberlain N.F.B. Sehested of Broholm and Addit surveyed an extensive area in the forest at Addit, south of Silkeborg. Here he found stone dykes made of fist-sized or slightly larger stones enclosing rectangular plots. Within the stone dykes, and especially alongside them, Sehested also found remains of pottery vessels; these were 'coarse, both large and small, often with fitted lugs'.

Sehested was in some doubt as to what he had found and he named the site Kirkegården (the Churchyard). Later it would become apparent that what he discovered was an extensive Iron Age field system, which he had surveyed in exemplary fashion. His successors have not held these extensive remains in such respect, and a few years ago they permitted the area to be ploughed in advance

Iron Age fields to the south of Tollund Man's find site, seen from the air. The photograph was taken shortly after the heath which previously covered the site was taken into cultivation. Pale shifting sand, which had drifted behind the Iron Age fences, reveals the outlines of the fields. *(Photo: Landinspektørernes Luftopmåling)*

of the planting of a new forest. Fortunately we still have Sehested's original survey data.

One of the few positive outcomes of the Second World War was a 'new' archaeological survey method which was put to use in Denmark: aerial photography.

In Western Jutland and parts of Central Jutland where the soil is poor and sandy there are good observational conditions for aerial archaeology. Where the soil has been well-manured, or where it has been turned so the roots can take a good hold, crops grow better and taller, and in oblique sunlight they cast a shadow which can be seen from the air.

Near Asklev, south of Bjældskovdal, within walking distance of where Tollund Man and Elling Woman were found, there is a large area laid waste by shifting sand. An aerial survey of the area in the 1950s and '60s led to the discovery of extensive areas covered in a mosaic pattern of rectangles framed by 'something white'. On the ground 'the white' proved to be shifting sand which had drifted behind the now vanished field banks. These were stone dykes like those found

An ard being drawn by oxen. Ards were in use from the Neolithic period until the Middle Ages. (Drawing: Flemming Bau)

by Sehested in Addit Skov, but out on the arable fields they had been removed when the heath was brought under cultivation. The white sand could still be seen years after the stones had been removed. Archaeologists were fortunate that these dykes were discovered in time because today's great agricultural machines now mix everything up so thoroughly that it is no longer possible to see Iron Age field systems from the air. It proved possible to measure the fields on the aerial photographs and they turned out to be very small, ranging from 25 x 25m to 50 x 200m.

Excavations of other field systems have revealed that ploughing was done with an 'ard', a wooden implement drawn by a pair of oxen, exactly as can be seen today in many countries where mechanised agriculture has yet to make inroads. Yokes for these oxen feature among the many wooden objects which peat cutters have found in Danish bogs.

The ard functioned like a single-toothed harrow in that it did not turn the soil in the way that a plough does, but drew a wide furrow. If the furrows were

'Seafood platter'. Mussels, cockles, oysters and other molluscs were gathered on the shore from Iron Age settlements located along the coasts – and cooked and eaten on the spot. *(Photo: Silkeborg Museum)*

At Lynderup, with a view of the Limfjord, Iron Age people had a 'kitchen midden' on the field sloping evenly down towards the water. *(Photo: Silkeborg Museum)*

close enough together, criss-crossing, the preparation of the soil corresponded to that achieved by using a plough. Finds of domestic refuse on the fields in the form of potsherds, pieces of fire-shattered stones and charcoal suggest that this waste material was used to fertilise the soil, along with what was mucked out from the byre.

At first glance the field boundaries look as if they were made from the stones thrown out from the field when it was cultivated, but the situation is not quite so simple. Sehested, and others who have excavated well-preserved field systems, have found pots associated with the dykes. These could have contained food for the people who were working the fields. Conversely, they could have held offerings of food placed to secure the goodwill of the gods for a bountiful harvest, on a par with the burying of vessels containing food by the posts which were to carry the roof of a house. The protection of the gods on both the house and the arable crops must have been held as equally important for the survival of the society.

Round heaps of stones by the fields, which are not burial sites but structures on or around which pots were placed, are very reminiscent of the heaps of stones found in bogs with their corresponding offerings of pots. In some fortunate instances it has been possible to see that these stone heaps were also furnished with a wooden figure such as Broddenbjerg Man from the Viborg area, the female figure from Forlev Nymølle near Skanderborg and the couple from Braak in Holstein.

The food which Tollund Man and other bog bodies had eaten might well lead one to believe that Iron Age people lived on a vegetarian diet in winter. Porridge (or gruel) was probably the daily fare all year round, and particularly towards the end of winter and in early spring it would perhaps have been the only food. The animals housed in the byre over winter were primarily intended for breeding, though it was probably possible to store the meat of autumn-slaughtered animals in either a smoked or dried form. In the granary at Overbygård bone remains were found which could derive from one or more hams hung from the ceiling. Milk was stored in the form of cheese. Pottery vessels, sieves and vessels with a large hole in the base were probably designed to separate the curds from the whey.

It has also become clear that kitchen middens, known in particular from the end of the Mesolithic period, were also an Iron Age phenomenon. Iron Age houses dating from Tollund Man's time have been excavated at Lynderup on Hjarbæk Fjord. Down by the fjord, only 200m away, were extensive kitchen middens. These constituted the waste material from meals of gathered oysters, mussels and other molluscs. The shell fish were cooked and eaten on the spot. Potboilers and thick layers of ash reveal that the cooking method involved heating stones on a fire until they glowed and then adding them to a cooking vessel to heat the water and the freshly collected shellfish; shortly afterwards the soup would be on the boil.

THE DEAD

It is a fundamental concept in many different cultures that the soul or spirit of the dead is released in conjunction with the conversion by fire of the dead body to smoke and burnt bone. It seems obvious to assume that this was also the case in Southern Scandinavia 3,000 years ago. There were transitional periods before and after the time when cremation was the exclusive burial practice when the two ways of dealing with the dead – cremation and inhumation – were practised side by side. There were also intermediary forms in which the burnt bones were placed in coffins and then treated like inhumations of entire bodies, including the use of grave goods and so on.

The burial tradition in the Celtic Iron Age was that everyone who died – apart from bog bodies – was burnt on a funeral pyre. The remains from the pyre were then crushed into small pieces and the mixture of burnt crushed bones and the remnants of the funeral pyre was placed in an urn or simply buried in a small pit.

A similar cremation tradition was also practised in the Late Bronze Age, but the burnt bone remains were not, as in the Iron Age, crushed after the fire had subsided.

Moreover, only a small part of the deceased's bones were actually buried, so either the mourners were not very careful in gathering up the remains after the fire, or they did not perceive this as being necessary – it was the symbolism which was important.

Southern Jutland has extensive Iron Age cemeteries, some containing as many as 1,500 burials. A low mound of earth covers each urn or the scant remains from the funeral pyre and the graves are often marked with a ring ditch. There is an air of uniformity about the graves, but it would probably be wrong to see this uniformity among the dead as reflecting equality among the living. Judging from the sizes of the farms in Iron Age villages, people were very probably not equal in life.

The grave goods were sparse, according to the practice of the time. They usually comprised small metal objects associated with clothing: pins or belt hooks – and very occasionally a neck ring. Objects which the deceased wore everyday in life followed them in death.

Further north on the Jutland peninsula, in Tollund Man's area, no corresponding cemeteries are in evidence. The burial grounds there are somewhat smaller and were probably used by a single family for a short period of a few generations.

The graves were covered with a circular flat stone packing, over which a low mound was thrown up. This was unlikely to be more than 10m in diameter; most were much less.

The crushing of the cremated bones means that today's human bone experts have great difficulties in determining the height, age and sex of the deceased.

Consequently, it is not possible to tell whether they were taller, shorter or of the same height as the bog bodies. It would be interesting to know whether the people who became bog bodies differed physically from the 'normal population', because theories have been proposed that those who were deposited in bog were the weak who were of no use in society.

Whether the clothing worn by the dead when they were burnt on the funeral pyre differed from that worn by the bog bodies is also a difficult matter to resolve. The few iron and bronze pins found among the remains of the funeral pyre could well have been used to fasten a skin cape at the front. Personal objects have also been found with some of the bog bodies, for example a bead and a small bronze disc. These objects are of a size which could be found and retrieved from the remains of the funeral pyre. They would originally have been worn as an ornament or an amulet about the neck or sewn into the clothing – but not specifically 'included' as grave goods. The bog bodies from Huldremose and Borremose 1946 both have neck ornaments and amulets of this kind. On the basis of the sparse finds left behind following cremation it seems unlikely that there was any real difference between ordinary people and those who ended up in the bog.

THE SMITH AND HIS RAW MATERIALS

In contrast to bronze, which was the dominant metal for edged tools and weapons in the Bronze Age, in the Iron Age, as the name suggests, iron became the preferred metal. Ornaments continued to be made of bronze, but tools intended to cut or stab were made of the new metal. It had always been necessary to import bronze, primarily from Central Europe. Iron on the other hand could be produced locally. The very first iron was probably imported, but local production quickly became established. However, it is evident well up into the Iron Age that swords, when they were to be of the very best quality, either came from foreign parts or were made of iron imported from the same sources. Whereas bronze could be melted and poured into moulds this was not possible with iron, but impurities could be smelted from the ore which was dug up. The iron resulting from the smelting process could be forged into knives, scythes, axes etc., and there is little doubt that people in Denmark had the ability to extract and work iron by about 500 BC. The melting point of iron – which is 1,528°C – was, however, first achievable only towards the end of the Middle Ages.

Traces of iron smelting in the form of slag are found almost everywhere that Iron Age people were active. The very earliest furnaces have yet to be found, but at

Bruneborg in Eastern Jutland archaeologists have come very close; the Bruneborg settlement dates from around 500 BC. The appearance of the smith's iron-smelting furnace was unfortunately not revealed at the site, but examples from elsewhere are able to provide additional information. The excavation did reveal the presence of slag and small pieces of iron next to the smith's forge. Forging requires the use of bellows in order to reach the temperature necessary for the iron to be worked. In order to prevent the heat radiated by the forge from damaging the bellows, and also to protect the person operating them, the bellows tip was covered by a plate: a 'tuyere', and this was found by the archaeologists. They also found quantities of bog iron, so the Iron Age smith did not have to go far to obtain his raw material. There was a wetland area probably no more than 600–800m away where bog iron could be found in quantity.

The next stage in the smelting process, 50kg of 'roasted' and crushed bog iron, lay ready. The remains of the furnace had been destroyed by modern ploughing, but it was of type known from other sites and is termed the Skovmark type. Like the smith's forge it required bellows in order to function optimally. Just a few centuries later – around the birth of Christ – the Skovmark furnace was replaced by a new furnace type in which the bellows were no longer necessary, at least not during the whole of the long period over which the smelting process extends.

The early furnaces had the form of a slightly conical shaft built of clay tempered with straw to render it heat resistant. The shaft was built over a pit in the ground. The pit was filled with clay, with a slag reservoir left open in the middle to receive the incandescent fluid that ran down from the furnace. At the front, the shaft had a 'door' closed with a plate in which there was a hole. It was through this hole the bellows supplied the furnace and its alternate layers of bog iron and charcoal or peat coal with oxygen-giving air, forcing the smelting temperature up to almost 1,300°C. The smelting process caused the impurities in the bog iron to become fluid so they ran down into the slag pit. The burning of the charcoal or peat coal also led to the formation of carbon monoxide which led to chemical reduction of the iron of the bog ore, actually in the form of iron oxide, to iron. The bog iron which was not sufficiently reduced, together with the impurities, formed the slag.

A large number of experiments have been carried out aimed at extracting iron in the Iron Age way. The results of this research show that it is exceptionally difficult to replicate the process and the quantities of 'modern' Iron Age iron which have been obtained are very modest. Silkeborg Museum has carried out a series of experiments and to date it has not proved possible to extract enough iron even to make a nail. Even a very short break in working the bellows brings the process to a halt, and it has not yet proved possible to restart it.

Experiments and calculations show that the total quantity of slag resulting from an extraction was about 10kg and the iron yield is presumed not to have exceeded 3kg. The consumption of charcoal or peat coal would have been about 15kg, plus about 5kg for pre-heating.

The Iron Age smith found bog iron on the edges of wetland areas where the soil had a degree of acidity, i.e. was non-calcareous and rich in humus. Rainwater normally percolates down through the soil and ultimately forms the ground water. However, if there are iron-rich minerals in the upper soil layers these become dissolved in the water and follow it on its path downwards. If, at some stage or in some way, the ground water again approaches the surface and comes into contact with oxygen in the air – for example in a bog or other wetland area – the iron in the water will react with the oxygen and precipitate out as a solid, limonite (brown iron ore), which can take several forms, most commonly ochre and bog iron.

The area where Tollund Man was found is renowned for its bog iron. The locality of Klode Mølle (klode = iron ingot) is visible from Bjældskovdal and in the Middle Ages the export of iron was one of Central Jutland's most important sources of income.

The use of charcoal as fuel is well known as the incompletely burnt pieces are easy for archaeologists to recognise in the field. The situation is rather different for corresponding pieces of peat coal. These readily disintegrate and quickly take the form of stained blotches of no discernible structure. However, it was an obvious possibility that the extraction of bog iron and the cutting of peat were combined in the same bog – these two important raw materials lay literally side by side.

It is likely, or at least possible, that the primary purpose of peat cutting during the Iron Age was to obtain peat coal for iron extraction and forging as both processes require a fuel with a greater capacity for heat production than ordinary firewood and peat.

According to a description from the nineteenth century, peat coal is made in almost the same way as charcoal:

> After drying, the peats are piled up to form a stack which is tightly sealed with turves so the oxygen supply can be regulated. Running through the turf-covered peat stack is a cavity which is filled with heather and some looser peat and then set alight. The peats ignite but the fire should never be allowed to become fiercer than the peats simply glow red throughout the process. This regulated combustion removes any remaining residual water, and substances such as tar either evaporate or seep down to the bottom of the stack. The material remaining at the end of the process is pure

carbon, which is easy to ignite, clean-burning and gives off few substances which can adversely affect the iron.

The coincidence between the incipient use of iron for tools and the increased peat cutting activity seen in bogs is unlikely to be pure serendipity. Could this coincidence also provide an explanation for the marked increase in the deposition of pots containing food in bogs? Do these represent offerings to the gods who provided people with these opportunities in the new Iron Age? Is this the reason that the greatest numbers of 'bog pots' are found in Jutland, where there are rich bog iron deposits and excellent supplies of raised bog peat?

9

TOLLUND MAN'S TRAVELS – A MIND JOURNEY

L et us suppose, for the sake of argument, that Tollund Man felt the urge to travel – either on foot or on horseback – all the way to the Mediterranean area and that on his journey he experienced a whole range of flourishing contemporary cultures.

We know that Jutland had contacts with areas as distant as the Black Sea. The Gundestrup Cauldron, which provides the best evidence, is thought to have been made there in the centuries just prior to AD 1. After its long journey, it ended up being deposited in the bog Rævemosen in Himmerland as an offering to the gods. But the links between two such distant places were probably very indirect – the cauldron could have passed through many hands.

Part of this thought experiment is that, without pedantic attention to precise historical details and dates, we can imagine his journey to have taken place in the Early Iron Age, within the time frame when radiocarbon dating says he most probably lived – between about 400 and 200 BC.

Having arrived safely in Athens in about 400 BC, the twenty-five year old Tollund Man would have immediately noticed the temple complex of the Acropolis with the Parthenon temple of marble at its centre. The temple was finished in 432 BC and covered a huge area of 69 x 31m. It contained the colossal gold and ivory statue of Athena. The fact that the man responsible for the statue and the decoration of the temple was called Pheidias is unlikely to have meant much to our Nordic traveller. For Tollund Man the distance to his own settlement's houses of clay, wood and thatch must have been simply beyond comprehension; at home there were no mighty marble columns and pillars to be seen – a couple of sturdy wooden posts was the closest they had.

The Acropolis. *(Photo: The Greek State Tourist Board)*

When walking around Athens at the foot of the Acropolis he might have managed to meet the philosopher Socrates whose ability to ask the right questions, and not answer, made him the father of ethics. In the process, Socrates made enemies who accused him of seducing youth. The People's Court sentenced him to death by drinking a deadly beaker of hemlock. Tollund Man was blissfully ignorant of the fact that, home again after his 'travels', he too would have to suffer a death ordained by others,

Tollund Man watched Olympic Games held in honour of the gods – discus-throwing, boxing and athletics – it involved the participation of naked men and women were naturally excluded. He saw the victory prize, an olive wreath, being placed around the neck of the man who had run fastest over the stadium's 192.27m.

He also experienced a Greek tragedy written by Sophocles and Euripides, sitting on the marble benches of the theatre.

Tollund Man still heard Greek spoken when he moved on to Italy, where Greek colonies had been established. This expansion into the Mediterranean had taken place in sharp competition with the Phoenicians and Etruscans, but after the Greeks had won command of the seas they established trading colonies.

In Italy, in the course of the fourth century BC, the Etruscans had also been subjugated by the Romans who expanded their territory out from the city of Rome, with its favourable location on the River Tiber.

Once in Rome, Tollund Man witnessed political discussions in the Senate and hear decisions about war, peace, economics and the Roman Empire's desire for expansion – decisions which in Rome's view were of consequence for the entire world – this was in the time of the Republic.

The letters SPQR were to be seen everywhere. Tollund Man came from Northern Europe where a further 600 years would elapse before the first runes were scratched on an ornament or a weapon. A Roman citizen had to explain it to him: SPQR was an abbreviation of Senatus Populusque Romanus, 'the Senate and the Roman People'. For Tollund Man it must have been completely incomprehensible; he was used to there just being the local chieftain, the man with the large farm in the village who made all such decisions. But then he came from a place where the soil and the village were at the centre of things, not a great city with its crafts and trade.

The Romans would have perceived Tollund Man as a Gaul. It was not until a couple of centuries after Tollund Man had ended up in the bog back home that Roman authors became aware of another people to the north of the territory of the Gauls: the Germans or Teutons.

After leaving Rome, Tollund Man could have headed north again, through the Po Valley and over the Alps to the far-reaching Celtic area which extended up into Central Europe, to where the Rhine and the Danube flow. What he noticed, first and foremost, were the remarkable ruins of town-like fortresses with their cemeteries. These had a few large burial mounds, each marking the grave of a person who had possessed unusual power and wealth. Until very recently, trade links with the Greek colony of Massalia (Marseille) had made these princes exceedingly rich. However, when the links became broken these large cities, whose economy was based on trade, proved to be just too big and they were forced to succumb; as a consequence, the local princes lost their power.

When the old social order disintegrated, large parts of the population had no option but to move on – migration and a new power structure were the consequences. A warrior class emerged which was in a position to mobilise many related tribes in joint military campaigns. The Romans received a foretaste of these in 387 BC when the Celts attacked and burnt Rome and the Celts would continue to harass them for almost 400 years.

These hard-hitting warriors were both horsemen and foot-soldiers. They were led by powerful chieftains who could steer the course of the battle from a war chariot pulled by a pair of horses. The warriors were drawn from different tribes, a situation which must have arisen from some system of mutual alliances.

Although Tollund Man probably saw some prosperity, there were no new towns, no fortresses or any extensive villages. On his journey through the mountain valleys he met people who lived scattered through the landscape. He watched a funeral and even from a distance there was no mistaking the furnishings which accompanied the deceased to the grave – he must have been a great warrior: a chariot and his personal weaponry accompanied the man to the next life. This was last funeral Tollund Man witnessed where the soul of the deceased was not released by the power of fire. On the rest of his journey north he encountered only burials of remains from the funeral pyre.

When he passed La Tène by Lake Neuchâtel in Western Switzerland he witnessed an unfathomable spectacle – hundreds of swords, matching the very best he had seen in his native country, were thrown out into the lake, together with shields, lances and parts of chariots. Some of the swords lay in magnificent, ornamented sheaths – with a form of decoration he saw everywhere the Celts lived or had been in contact with. Visibly shaken, he watched all these wonderful items disappear for ever beneath the water as offerings to a deity. He had no idea that as he approached his homeland, at Hjortspring on Als, he would be able to see a similar spectacle – in which weapons, including a war canoe, wooden shields, spears and swords, were offered in exactly the same way. He kept his distance from the scene and never discovered whether this sacrificed weaponry was taken from an enemy who had landed nearby, or whether it constituted the spoils of plunder brought home from a faraway place. Whatever the source, these items were all being offered to the war god to ensure that the battle also went in favour of the local warriors on their next encounter.

Everything was thrown into the lake from two long wooden jetties and the weaponry was accompanied by animals: oxen, pigs and horses. People were also sacrificed – thrown into the lake. One had a halter of hemp rope around his neck.

On the shore of the lake, he caught sight of a beautifully carved double yoke for a pair of oxen. At home they used yokes that were exactly the same. The thought occurred to him that the familiar items at home perhaps came from this place, although trade in wooden objects over such a long distance did not seem likely. But he had also seen the rectangular wooden shields before and then there were the same turned wooden bowls that his people were not able to make for themselves and which travelling merchants brought from the south.

Tollund Man continued northwards and, almost imperceptibly, the language changed character – he was approaching his native country. Throughout his journey he had dressed in local attire. This was most practical, whether it was a matter of keeping himself warm or cool. Now he wore a skin cape like everyone

The Celtic migration, as seen by Flemming Bau.

else. He could shave and cut his hair as required, so he didn't stand out from the crowd. He had kept his hair short throughout the journey but at one point, shortly before the land narrowed, he encountered a possible problem in fitting in. The hairstyle of the local Swabian men required long hair which could be gathered together and tied in a knot at one side of the head.

The houses, the fields, the cemeteries and the smell of smoke from the many fires told him that he was on the right track. The language, which had changed enormously since he left the mountains, he could now understand, albeit with some difficulty. So far on his journey he had heard Greek, Etruscan, Latin and Celtic.

He was also fortunate in being in the company of people who followed a road that led up the middle of the country so he didn't have to cross rivers and wetlands. His fellow travellers were on their way north carrying merchandise from the south: luxury items such as metal cauldrons, ornaments, bronze for casting, weapon parts, weapons, even entire wagons. On the way they passed people travelling in the opposite direction who were carrying wares such as skins and salt.

They all followed the same road, the one which eventually led across Bjældskovdal, and here Tollund Man's journey came to an end.

10

A CHANGE OF RELIGION

T he transition from Bronze Age to Iron Age was much more than just the replacement of bronze with iron for edged tools such as knives, axes, swords and sickles. Multiple changes in lifestyle and religion also took place.

Religion has for many years been virtually taboo in Danish archaeology and if there was a possibility of explaining something in terms of a 'thin' rational explanation rather than an obvious irrational/cultic act, the 'thin' but rational option was always preferred.

The Bronze Age Sun Chariot is, however, difficult to explain as anything other than a cultic object. Following intensive research, archaeologist Flemming Kaul has now convincingly reconstructed elements of the beliefs and religion of Bronze Age people. On the basis of archaeological artefacts, rock carvings and engravings on especially, razors, he has been able to unveil a religion which centred on the sun and its passage across the sky. Based on Bronze Age iconography, it seems there was a perception of a daily cycle whereby, in the morning, the sun is helped by a fish from a 'night ship' to a 'day ship'. A horse then collects the sun from the ship at midday and passes it on to another ship, after which a snake gathers the sun from this ship and helps it set, hidden in the curl of its tail. The night ship, with the hidden sun, then sails through the night until the fish again offers its assistance in the morning.

It was not just a matter of the sun being an object of worship, but the belief that behind the sun and, consequently, the physical world there was a higher cosmic force. The sun's course – a cyclical movement – was linked to the passage of the year and, accordingly, became intrinsically linked with agricultural religions in which the seasons were of critical importance. In this form of religion the afterlife of the deceased is presumed to be linked to the sun and the natural cycle.

Could the many depictions of human figures seen in the rock carvings represent gods? Examples show that this is unlikely to be the case – they are more likely to be ordinary people, depicted as participants in ritual events and acts. Some are carrying an image of the sun; others are wearing horned helmets, lifting oxen high into the air or blowing into lures.

Flemming Kaul goes as far as to suggest that the period 'Bronze Age' should be renamed 'Sun Age'. This sun religion had a very wide geographical distribution encompassing the Scandinavian Peninsula, Denmark and Northern Germany. Three thousand years ago, a common fundamental understanding prevailed over large parts of Europe, despite significant cultural differences.

Razor from the Late Bronze Age bearing a 'sun ship' motif. (Photo: Silkeborg Museum)

The end of the Bronze Age heralded new times – the gods took on human form. One of them is Broddenbjerg Man – an idol with human features found in 1881 during peat cutting in a small bog, Broddenbjerg Mose, near Viborg. (Today the bog forms part of a golf course where the find site, now a lake, continues to receive 'offerings' in the form of golf balls from unfortunate golfers.)

The 88cm high figure is of oak; two branches form the legs and a side branch represents an over-sized penis. The upper part of the main trunk has been carved into the form of a very characteristic and sternly inscrutable face. Pitch had been smeared at the root of the penis and at its tip.

With its heavy accentuation of the male member, the figure – like the bog bodies – posed an ethical problem for the National Museum, though in this case it was more of a moral dilemma: could the idol be exhibited? The answer for many years was 'no!' – school pupils and other impressionable souls visited the museum! The fact that he – like the bog bodies – was of great scientific value and, as a museum exhibit, simply unsurpassed, was steadfastly ignored. In contrast to the bog bodies he was, however, conserved and could be seen – by the initiated – in the museum's stores.

The Broddenbjerg figure was found standing upright in the bog, very close to its edge. Directly beside him was a heap of about 200 stones, each no bigger than it could be moved with one hand, as the excavator A. Feddersen so vividly describes it. Among the stones were sherds from at least four pottery vessels. The combination of the wooden figure, the stone heap and the vessels, which probably contained food offerings, can hardly be interpreted in any other way than as a place where rituals were performed.

Two spiral arm rings and a neck ring of bronze with ship motifs on the oval terminals had previously been found in the bog. These date from the end of the Late Bronze Age and are probably contemporary with, or slightly earlier than, the figure, the stone heap and the pottery vessels. A radiocarbon analysis of the figure gave a date of 760–410 BC. Archaeologists were fortunate in this respect as the chemicals used in conserving the figure had made it impossible to obtain a radiocarbon date for the wood itself. However, it did prove possible to date the pitch which was smeared on the figure at the root of his penis as the lump of pitch had fallen off prior to conservation and was stored untreated.

The Broddenbjerg finds illustrate, in the best possible way, the transition from the sun cult of the Bronze Age – the neck ring showing the ship which sails across the firmament – to the Iron Age's worship of anthropomorphic gods – the wooden figure.

Broddenbjerg Man found in a bog south-east of Viborg. The figure was found together with offerings next to a round heap of stones. *(Photo: Silkeborg Museum)*

A stone heap (*horgr*) as a footing for Broddenbjerg Man. *(Reconstruction drawing: Margrethe Petrine Jensen)*

The fact that Broddenbjerg Man probably sat 'enthroned' on top of the stone heap is confirmed by another discovery made at Hobro.

Towards the end of the nineteenth century, during peat cutting in a bog at Rosbjerggård, north of Hobro, many remains were found of offerings dating from the Late Bronze Age and Early Iron Age. These comprised scattered finds of metal vessels imported from Italy and remains of pottery vessels as well as two large, and several smaller, domed stone heaps. From beneath and over these heaps came finds of numerous potsherds, a drinking horn and cow's horn.

Sophus Müller, who was the National Museum's fraught director at the time, was forced to admit that:

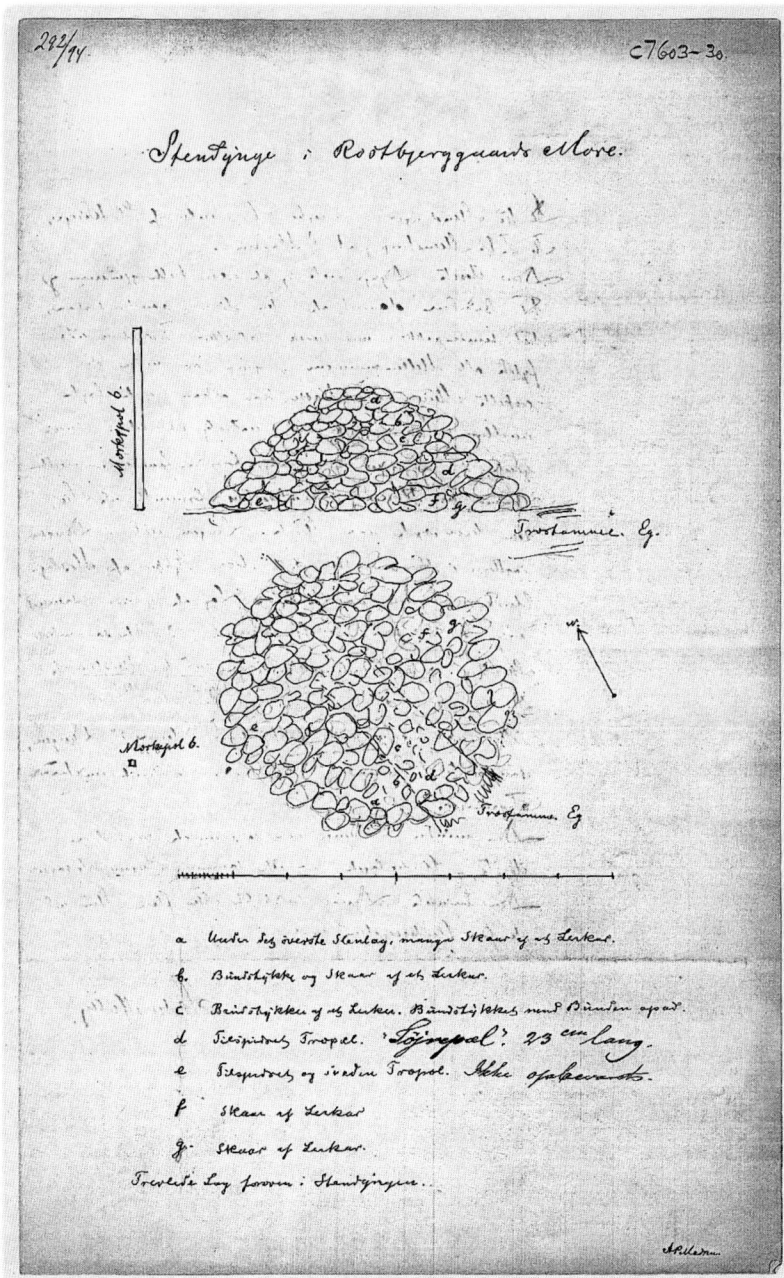

Two pieces of wood, found in the top of a heap of stones where offerings had been left, are interpreted as the legs of a figure like that from Broddenbjerg. Rosbjerggård near Hobro. *(Drawing: A.P. Madsen, the National Museum)*

There is no other explanation on offer for these stone heaps than that they are altars. All that is lacking is an idol. However, uppermost on the largest altar stood two thick pieces of wood, carved to a point at one end and decayed at the other. Could these not be the feet of one such ... the pieces of wood lying obliquely on top of the heap.

In support of this perception is that, in a bog near Viborg, a well-preserved 88cm high, carved wooden figure has been encountered standing on a stone heap of the same shape and size as that mentioned here. The head is very carefully carved; but the figure is without arms and downwards it ends in two pointed stakes of the same kind as those mentioned above. The figure [Broddenbjerg Man] is strongly phallic and therefore undoubtedly a depiction of a deity, probably dating from an early part of the Iron Age.

As already mentioned, the radiocarbon analysis provided a slightly earlier date in the Late Bronze Age.

Stone heaps, with associated finds of wooden figures, are also known from Forlev Nymølle near Skanderborg and Braak in Holstein. In both of these instances the heap and the figure are dated to the Early Iron Age. Pots containing food and other objects had been placed by the stone heaps and by the figures.

These particular stone heaps are, as already mentioned, generally rounded in shape and as the pottery vessels and objects lie scattered among the stones it seems likely that the heaps are the result of a combination of ordinary deposition and throwing.

All things considered, a heap of stones could have had various functions through history – it may have resulted from field clearance, been a signpost, a cairn or the remains of a burial place. The term *harg* is known from Gotland and is used in common parlance in reference to heaps of stones which have been built on the coast to serve as navigation marks. The combination of stone heap, wooden figure and offerings often prompts use of the word *hørg*, but in a different context. In Old Norse poetry and prose there are examples of *horgr* being used in reference to heaps of stones which were gathered by human hand and which are associated with cultic activities. The most important example of these is usually identified as a verse from the Eddic poem 'Hyndluljoth' ('Poem of Hyndla') where the goddess Freyja praises her favourite Ottar: 'For me a shrine [*horgr*] of stones he made,' (Henry Adams Bellows (trans.) *The Poetic Edda* (New York, 1923)). That reference is being made to a stone heap or stone altar appears immediately clear.

The fact that stone heaps on land, for example those found associated with prehistoric fields, also constituted a 'footing' for one or more wooden figures seem

Bog pots found during recent excavations of a sacrificial area in the bog Fuglsøgårds Mose. *(Photo: Museum Østjylland, Randers)*

an obvious possibility, but the lack of suitable conditions for preservation make it impossible to verify this.

The most important aspect of the offerings was not the pottery vessels themselves but the food they contained: dairy products, grain or meat. Offerings of cattle have also been found: skin, skull and bones.

Many pots have turned up during peat cutting, some singly, others in large groups, and sometimes associated with other types of object and scattered bones, revealing that human sacrifices also took place from time to time. Single pots could, of course, have been left behind by prehistoric peat cutters. However, most 'bog pots', as they are collectively termed, served cultic purposes. The dating of the pots leaves no doubt that this activity particularly took place during the Early Iron Age. The peat cutters from Bjældskovdal recalled that during their work in the bog they had encountered pottery vessels on several occasions, but none of these appears to have been recorded by a museum. There are official records of over 200 'bog pot' localities in Denmark, but this is clearly only a fraction of those encountered by peat cutters.

The numerous cast spiral bronze neck rings, dating from the end of the Bronze Age and in particular the Early Iron Age, are also votive gifts.

The offerings dating from around the time of Tollund Man and Elling Woman also mark changed perceptions in the mythology. The objects found deposited in bogs now also include small bronze female figures wearing neck rings – in pairs like those which were offered. These bronze figures tell of a belief in a female deity; the rings are her symbol.

Chronologically, the change in religion coincided with the sacrifices of humans who later became bog bodies.

11

GATHERING THE THREADS

In 1996 the opportunity came about for detailed study of the best-known bog bodies from north-west Europe – they were quite literally brought together for an exhibition at Silkeborg Museum. It was the idea of the Dutch bog body expert Wijnand van der Sanden, and the exhibition should originally have taken place in The Netherlands, at Drents Museum in van der Sanden's home town. However, problems with the loan of Tollund Man, among others, resulted in Silkeborg becoming the place where the exhibition plans became a reality. The exhibition enabled visitors to stand face to face not only with our own Danish bog bodies and skeletons, but also with the German Osterby Man, Windeby Girl and Roter Franz. Material about Lindow Man came from England and Drents Museum loaned Yde Girl and the two men from Weerdinge.

The ethical and aesthetical aspects of producing an exhibition of bog bodies prompted their share of sleepless nights for the exhibition organiser (the author). Neither was the local newspaper's advanced coverage supportive, proclaiming 'Ligtræf' ('Corpse Rally'). The mayor's enthusiasm for the project was similarly rather lukewarm. But fortune smiled on the exhibition when the opening speaker, the Irish poet Seamus Heaney, who had written the poem 'The Tollund Man' in the museum's visitors' book in 1973, was awarded the Nobel Prize for Literature (1995) in recognition of, among others, that very poem.

The year after he had written the poem in the museum's visitors' book, Seamus Heaney met Professor P.V. Glob, who by that time had left the Aarhus Museum – and Grauballe Man – to become Keeper of National Antiquities and Director of the National Museum in Copenhagen. Heaney has often said that Glob's book *The Bog People* was a hugely important source of inspiration in his poetry.

Following his meeting Heaney wrote a letter to a Danish student at Cambridge University in which he stated 'P.V. Glob treated me to one of his home-brewed beers in a dusty backroom of the Copenhagen Museum in 1974. I felt I was baptised a Dane at that moment.'

The Irish poet Seamus Heaney was awarded the Nobel Prize for Literature in 1995; his main works include 'The Tollund Man'. Heaney opened Silkeborg Museum's bog body exhibition '*Ansigt til ansigt*' (Face to Face) in 1996. *(Photo: Jan Cavling)*

When the Danish Queen Margrethe II also expressed a wish to take part in the exhibition opening, the organiser could begin to concentrate on the actual exhibition content and its scientific statement. An exhibition normally presents the end results of academic research but here it was actually possible to conclude scientific results from the exhibition itself.

When the exhibition closed it became clear to me that the only thing the bog bodies on display had in common was the fact that they had been deposited in a preserving bog. They extended in date from the Mesolithic almost up to modern times. And if all those involved had had their way, the exhibition would have included corpses from the nineteenth century. But here, as the responsible organiser, I had to draw the line. Exhibiting the bodies of people whose names were known transgressed my own ethical limits.

On their discovery, several of the bog bodies were exceptionally well preserved, but methods of conservation were not always adequate so conservators often had to resort to reconstruction of the body. The exhibition demonstrated very clearly that the corpse then became as the conservator believed it must have appeared, and, in the same way, the message or story which could be deduced from it saw expression in the finished result.

The striking face of Broddenbjerg Man. *(Photo: Silkeborg Museum)*

A missing lower jaw on Osterby Man, the corpse with the characteristic Swabian knot, was replaced by another jaw from another find. This gave the man an unintentional undershot jaw and a rather fierce demeanour.

The exhibition also showed examples of the imaginative stories concocted about the bog bodies, often with political undertones. This applies to the German bog bodies found in the years following the collapse of the Third Reich, when it was still possible to find traces of 'Germanic virtues'. The interpretation of Windeby Girl as the young daughter of a prominent family who, through fornication, had besmirched the family's honour and had, as a consequence, had been executed and laid in Domlandsmoor, near her lover, proved to be pure fantasy. 'She' was very probably a thirteen-year-old boy who, when alive, suffered periods of illness and hunger and who died a natural death.

The facial expressions of bog bodies were made more 'interesting' and rather less terrifying than the sight which met their discoverers following many years in the bog.

The exhibition also included examples of the many other human sacrifices which had taken place, accompanied by artefacts such as parts of wagons. Those sacrificed were most often laid out on the surface of a bog or sunk in a lake together with various artefacts. These events generally took place later than the Celtic Iron Age, i.e. when the bog bodies had their heyday. They differ from the bog bodies in that the latter were usually deposited individually in a peat cutting, accompanied by no other items than clothes which they very probably were wearing at the time.

The exhibition also revealed that children were represented in the finds from abroad; something that is not seen in Denmark. Only in the case of Borremose Man 1946 were the upper halves of a humerus and a tibia of a child found associated with the corpse. These lay in half a pottery vessel by the left knee of the body. It is uncertain how they should be interpreted.

It was clear that the Danish bog bodies almost all dated from the Early Iron Age – the Celtic Iron Age – with a small degree of overlap before and after.

Another striking common feature was that the bodies were clothed in a skin cape or had one or more pieces of clothing placed by them. Even the severed heads found at Roum and Osterby in Schleswig were wrapped in a skin cape. Only Grauballe Man lacked either cape or other clothing.

Deposition in the bog in a sleeping position, as in the case of Tollund Man, or wrapped in skin capes, in the case of others, clearly suggests that the bog bodies were sacrificed as part of a cultic act – they were not criminals who had simply to be disposed of.

The next question was: Who were the gods to whom the bog bodies were sacrificed? In an attempt to provide an answer, Silkeborg Museum organised an exhibition 'Gods of the Bog' in 2001. The fact that anthropomorphic – human-like – figures have been found in the bogs of north-west Europe is well-known and well-documented in the archaeological literature.

Some common features reveal that these figures were more than just random carvings; figures such as those from Broddenbjerg, Forlev Nymølle and Braak were involved in cultic activities.

In a more detailed examination of Broddenbjerg Man, carried out by the author, an 'engraving' around the neck proved to be an actual carved, narrow furrow which ended in an upward obtuse angle at the back of the neck. When shown the result of this investigation, a pathologist was able to confirm the striking similarity to a hanging furrow. An interpretation of the furrow as denoting a neck ring is rather less likely as this would hardly have appeared as being cut into the wood. It is tempting to see a link between hanging and the fact that the figure has a phallic appearance, but further examples would be required in order to explore this possibility.

The wooden figures must be depictions of the gods themselves – gods with human features – were these the forerunners of the Ases of the Nordic mythology?

Consequently, a third exhibition, 'Ragnarok – The World of Odin', which took place in 2005 focussed on the Nordic gods. The overall aim of this exhibition was to trace the belief in the Ases back in time and discover its roots, which perhaps extended as far back as these wooden figures.

The exhibition began with what we know – the literary descriptions of the Ase religion found in the Icelandic sagas. The Rend Adam of Bremen and Revd Thietmar of Merseburg also described – naturally from their Christian point of view – the cult of the Nordic gods.

Through archaeological artefacts, picture stones, tapestries and iconography this religion could then be traced, step by step, back through time. Well-known but characteristic stories associated with the Ase religion, such as the death of Balder, Odin's magical blowing in the ear of Balder's horse, could be shown to have been known as far back as the fifth century AD. Bracteates from this time have these stories as motifs, but these depictions are the oldest on artefacts which we definitely know were not imported.

Runic inscriptions, which appear after the second century AD, were not much assistance as they simply represent owner's names or invocations we are unable to understand today. Consequently, they provided little opportunity to trace the history of the Ase religion.

About 1,000 years earlier, towards the end of the Bronze Age, an iconography blossomed which was closely linked with cult activities. However, the difference between this and the imagery of the Iron Age, as it appeared at the beginning of the fifth century AD, is so great that there must have been a change in religion in the intervening period; this probably took place around 500 BC.

There appears to be a clear link between the cessation of Bronze Age sun worship, and the rituals associated with it, and the changes in the structure of society which are apparent in the archaeological record: settlement pattern, agriculture, iron extraction, peat cutting, burial practices and offerings.

By the time the iconography reappeared at the beginning of the fifth century AD, the Ase religion was already a reality. The scattered infant roots of this belief are perhaps to be found back at the beginning of the Iron Age, when the various

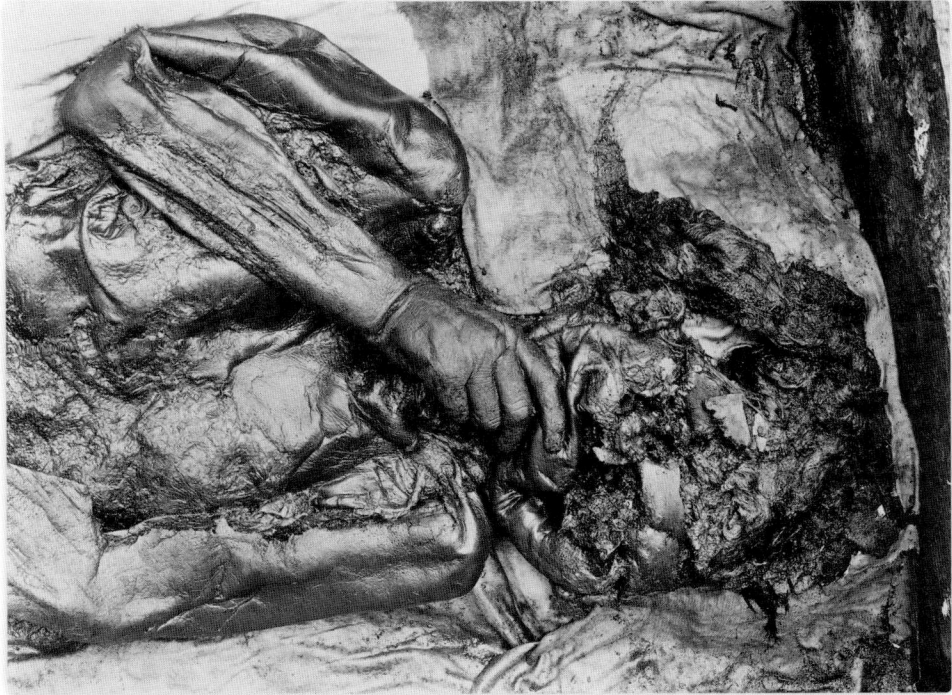

The weight of the peat and the movement of the bog cause deformation. Borremose Woman's head is heavily compressed. This was previously thought to be the result of violence associated with deposition in the bog. *(Photo: The National Museum)*

elements that later converged to form what we now call the Ase religion could have been drawn from near and far.

There were extensive networks of contacts across Europe in the Early Iron Age. An exemplary illustration is provided by the Gundestrup Cauldron – and its 9kg of pure silver – found during peat cutting in the bog Rævemosen in Western Himmerland. The cauldron's distant origin has always been the subject of discussion. It is now believed to have been made by the Thracians, a people who lived on the Black Sea coast in about 100 BC. The imagery with which the cauldron is decorated refers to the world of the Celtic gods: We recognise, among others, the Celtic horned god Cernunnos and people blowing the characteristic instrument, the carnyx. The costumes and ornaments (the neck rings) are Celtic, and an offering scene shows one of the great sacrificial cauldrons in use.

Some elements of the Ase religion, for example the idea of the world-tree, are extremely complex, but this concept is found in the Greek world synchronously with the Early Iron Age in Denmark.

The idea behind the tree must be extremely ancient and this has allowed it to develop in many different directions. There are nevertheless a number of characteristic common features revealing a common origin.

Human sacrifice comprises one of the important elements of the Ase religion, where hanging is part of the cult ceremony – precisely the fate which must have befallen Tollund Man and Elling Woman.

THE HANGED

Tollund Man was hanged, Elling Woman was hanged, Borremose Man 1946 was hanged or strangled, the skeleton from Lykkegårds Mose was found with a rope about its neck, Huldremose Woman had a band wound around her neck, perhaps her own hair band. The man from Krogens Møllemose had a plaited leather halter bound with a knot. Alongside Borremose Man 1947 lay a leather cord with a loop around the corpse's neck and a further cord by his legs, Daugbjerg Man had a rope at his waist and the bog body found beside Windeby Girl had a loop of plant fibre around his neck.

Of the other Danish bog bodies from the Celtic Iron Age it has only proved possible to establish the cause of death in one case: Grauballe Man. His throat was cut from ear to ear. He already differed by being the only Danish bog body apparently laid in a bog completely naked – the others were clothed in some way or had clothes placed beside them or in the near vicinity.

The extreme brutal violence which is evident from Grauballe Man and the majority of other bog bodies, and which to date has been seen as the cause of death or a contributory factor, can now be explained in terms of the pressure exerted by the bog. This crushed the bones gradually as they were attacked by the acids of the bog. Meanwhile the weight of the peat became ever greater as the bog steadily grew.

The idea that Tollund Man and Elling Woman were hanged from sacred trees as sacrifices to Odin, or another deity who appears later in history in the form of Odin, is challenging.

The hanging cult is linked to the god Odin of Ase religion. Icelandic scalds gave him the byname Hangaguð or Hangatýr which means 'God of the Hanged'.

The account of Odin on the tree is to be found in Hávamál ('The Words of Odin the High One') (reproduced in its entirety in Codex Regius, also referred to as 'The King's Book', written down in about 1200 by Icelander Snorre Sturluson).

> I trow I hung on that windy Tree
> nine whole days and nights,
> stabbed with a spear
> offered to Odin,
> myself to mine own self given,
> high on that Tree of which none hath heard
> from what roots it rises to heaven.
>
> (Olive Bray (trans.), *Hávamál – Wisdom for Wanderers
> and Counsel to Guests* (London, 1908))

This poem has often been seen as a description of a typical offering to Odin, established by the god himself, but must for good reason more probably be perceived as part of an initiation ritual, especially as the subject is seen to return to life from death.

Another written source about the hanging cult of the Ase religion is provided by the German canon Adam of Bremen, who writes that:

> ... of every living thing that is male, they offer nine heads, with the blood of which it is customary to placate gods of this sort. The bodies they hang in the sacred grove that adjoins the temple. Now this grove is so sacred in the eyes of the heathen that each and every tree in it is believed divine ...
>
> (Adam of Bremen, *History of the Archbishops of Hamburg-Bremen*,
> translation, notes and introduction by Francis J. Tschan (New York, 2002))

A similar account referring to Lejre, near Roskilde, given by Thietmar, Bishop of Merseburg (*c.* AD 1000), suggests that offerings to sacred trees took place in a corresponding fashion. Religious historians are of the opinion that there is little doubt that the hanged were sacrificed to Odin.

TAPESTRIES AND PICTURE STONES

Archaeological artefacts, older than the Icelandic sagas and dating from pagan times, continue the account of hanging as a part of cult activities.

There is a tapestry from the famous ship burial at Oseberg in Vestfold, Norway, which shows a grove festooned with hanged people. The tapestry lay in what is thought to be the grave of Harald the Fair-haired's grandmother, Queen Åsa, who

The Oseberg Tapestry from around AD 800. This was placed in the ship burial at Oseberg by Oslo Fjord. The tapestry shows a grove with hanged human sacrifices, probably offerings to Odin. *(Copyright: The Museum of Cultural History, University of Oslo. Photo: Eirik Irgens Johnsen)*

Offering scene showing seven hanged individuals. Picture stone from Bote on Gotland, c. AD 700. *(Photo: The National Historical Museum, Stockholm)*

died in the mid-ninth century, i.e. in pagan times. The fact that hanged people were employed as a motif on a tapestry and that this motif was seen as being so important that it should accompany the deceased to the next life, underlines the central role of hanging in the Ase religion.

A Gotlandic picture stone from the locality of Lärbro, apparently dating from the eighth century and erected as a grave monument over a chieftain, shows a hanging scene with which Odin's name can possibly be linked. The scene appears to illustrate the legend of Starkad. In brief, the story goes that Odin demanded the sacrifice of a man from King Vikar's army in return for fortune in battle. Lots were drawn and the king himself drew the fateful lot. The king allowed himself to undergo a 'mock-hanging', but the hanging became a reality when Odin persuaded the giant Starkad to take his side. The rope which – unknown to Odin – held Vikar on the ground was pierced by Starkad's spear as he uttered: 'Now I give you to Odin'. The tree held down by the rope, ensuring that the noose about Vikar's neck remained loose, suddenly straightened, tightening the noose and Vikar became a hanging sacrifice to Odin.

Another picture stone from Bote shows a whole series of hanged people; seven in all, suspended from a branch.

Naked Wearing a Belt

If we attempt to go even further back in time, to the sixth and seventh centuries AD, the gold fogeys (small sheet-gold figures for cultic use) of this period include small stylised figures depicting ritual hangings and naked individuals, some wearing a belt exactly like Tollund Man.

The figures are identified as having been hanged by the fact that their arms and over-sized hands hang loosely by their sides. Their legs also dangle, with the feet hanging downwards, slightly bent or straight like a dancer's. A few scholars have also expressed the view that these were participants in a ritual dance. In most cases those depicted are men, but figures wearing brooches high on their chest could be women. It is clear that they are naked, and some have a neck ring or a noose about their neck. These details were produced by pressing, engraving or by bending gold thread around the neck of the figure. The figures have been found at, among other places, Sorte Muld on Bornholm, Uppåkra near Lund in Scania and Lundeborg near Svendborg – all sites which, in terms of material culture, rise above the rest of society.

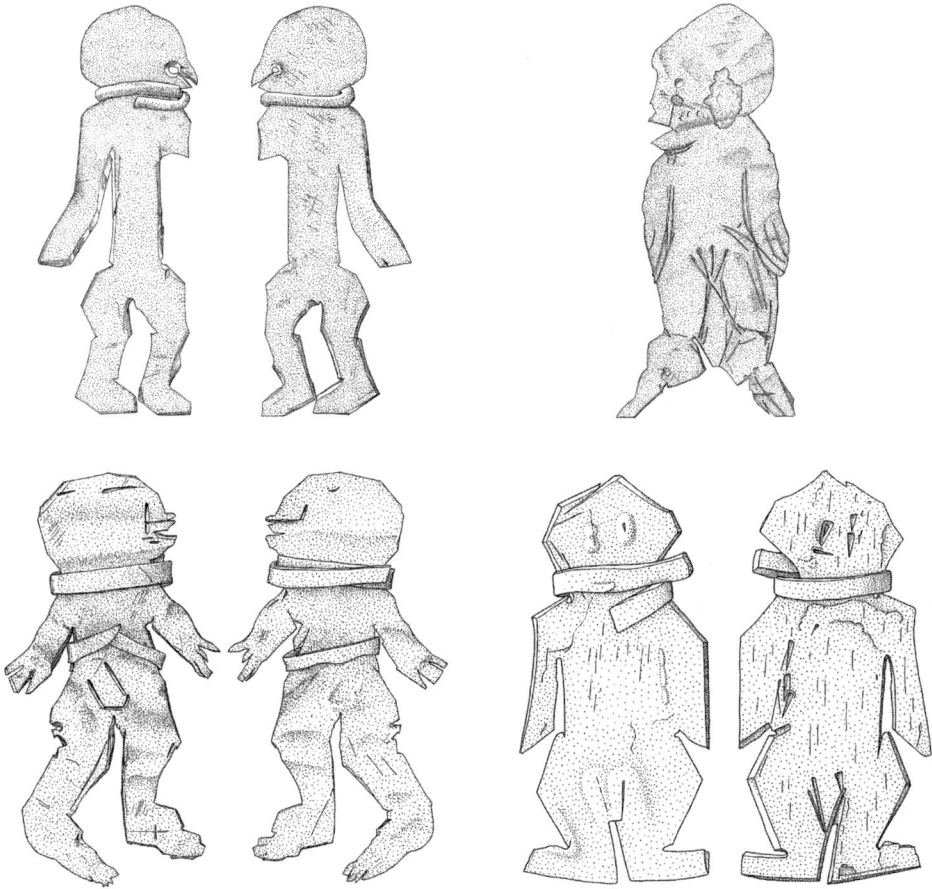

Gold fogeys, naked with a belt and neck ring or hanging furrow, from Sorte Muld on Bornholm. *(Drawing: Eva Koch)*

An interesting parallel is seen in the little gold man from Slipshavn Skov near Nyborg. The gold figure is naked, has marked genitalia and an over-sized, rounded and almost child-like head with large circular eyes and an open mouth. He is wearing a very characteristic gold neck ring with overlapping ends. The figure also has arms which appear to hang loosely by the side of his body and his hands are clasped, but with protruding thumbs; a feature also seen in the people who have been hanged.

A period of between 400 and 800 years separates the earliest artefacts showing figures related to a hanging cult from the hanged bog bodies. Even so, the way in which they were deposited in the bog suggests that Tollund Man and Elling Woman were sacrificed as part of a cultic ceremony in which hanging and strangulation were widely practised.

To say that Tollund Man and Elling Woman were sacrificed to Odin would be to go too far, because the archaeological record does not presently provide evidence for the Ase religion having been established at such an early point in the Iron Age. It is, however, very likely that established ritual activities and ceremonies can continue and become integrated into a new religion, where they have a significant role. We are able to find numerous examples of this in the transition from paganism to Christianity.

Tollund Man, like Elling Woman, hanged as a sacrifice to the gods! *(Photo: Robert Clark)*

The riddle is solved!

P.S. In continuation of the above train of thought, it is gratifying that a hill close to Tollund Man's find site bears the name Vonsbjerg (Odin's hill) and that the finders of the bog body came from Tollund (Thor's grove); these are names which are mentioned in the Middle Ages and which probably go much further back in time.

> ... In the end I gathered
> From the display-case peat my staying powers,
> Told my webbed wrists to be like silver birches,
> My old uncallused hands to be young sward,
> The spade-cut skin to heal, and got restored
> By telling myself this. Late as it was,
> The early bird still sang, the meadow hay
> Still buttercupped and daisied, sky was new.
> I smelled the air, exhaust fumes, silage reek,
> Heard from my heather bed the thickened traffic
> Swarm at a roundabout five fields away
> And transatlantic flights stacked in the blue.

(From Seamus Heaney's 'The Tollund Man in Springtime'
in *District and Circle*, Faber and Faber, London 2006)

INDEX